The Vaulted Room

Daniele Iozzia

The Vaulted Room

Essays on Aesthetics

Logos Verlag Berlin

λογος

Bibliographic information published by the Deutsche Nationalbibliothek

The Deutsche Nationalbibliothek lists this publication in the Deutsche Nationalbibliografie; detailed bibliographic data are available on the Internet at http://dnb.d-nb.de .

ISBN 978-3-8325-4678-6

Cover image: Design for a small bedroom in café-au-lait and powder blue. Watercolour by Daniele Iozzia.

Logos Verlag Berlin GmbH
Comeniushof, Gubener Str. 47,
D-10243 Berlin
Germany

Tel.: +49 (0)30 / 42 85 10 90
Fax: +49 (0)30 / 42 85 10 92
http://www.logos-verlag.com

Contents

INTRODUCTION

A vaulted room, however small or vast, replicates at a domestic level the experience of being under the sky, in a way which can be measured, controlled, and which shelters. Any intellectual research reduces a world which is exhilarating and fascinating but also obscure and arcane, to a more definable size. Human creation too is a world that is difficult to grasp, and therefore by analyzing it we might need to adapt it to our own level of understanding. Aesthetics as a discipline is a vaulted room, which replicates on a more familiar and manageable level certain aspects of the external reality and of human expression. This small collection of essays deals with various issues related to the history of aesthetics from antiquity to the modern day, with a view to raising some questions and focusing on scholarly research through a specific aesthetic lens.

Callimachus of Cyrene, a poet, and Plotinus, a philosopher, are apt subjects for such an approach, as they both have a peculiar place in the history of aesthetics and had an impact on the art and the reflection of their times but also of later periods. In the case of Plotinus, in particular, his influence extends to many centuries later. Philological and philosophical knowledge are here combined in the reconstruction of the aesthetic interest of different ages not only philosophically, but also with an eye to the results of the artistic production.

The first of the essays presented here investigates Callimachus' position on poetry and his knowledge of Plato's and Aristotle's writings. In particular, it is more than likely that Callimachus knew the Socratic school of Cyrene, his hometown, as foreshadowed in a passage from his *Aitia* about the validity of the auditory and cognitive experience in opposition to other forms of pleasures.

The second essay focuses on the problem of when precisely a work of art should be considered finished. This question is particularly pressing in relation to the creative process and that is the reason why, during the Renaissance, artists and thinkers reflected on what would be more important for the artistic result. This paper investigates the possibility of finding links between the attitude of artists and writers to the different degrees of refinement and revision of their work, and their engagement with Neoplatonic ideas and culture.

Plotinus' views on the ethical response to human beauty are scrutinized in the third essay, which focuses on a passage from his first treatise on providence. Here Plotinus discusses the different reactions of Paris and Idomeneus with respect to the beauty of Helen, thus leading to a reflection on individual responsibility within the erotic and aesthetic experience.

The fourth essay deals with an altogether different subject, which might be even somewhat controversial in an academic context. Here, in fact, I choose to focus on a very narrow field, that of interior design and decoration, which is very little studied but of great potential for its applications. The focus will be in particular on a category that is more neglected than others, namely that of classic or traditional residential interiors, with a reflection on the activity of Renzo Mongiardino.

Two essays consist of material that I have already published in Italian, but everything has been revised, updated and substantially rewritten.[1] The reason for putting together these seemengly different papers is primarily related to the pleasure that I had in writing them. If this sounds like a superficial motivation, we must reconsider the basis for Callimachus' poetic effort. He does not find pleasure in the transient titillation of the body but in the perennial acquisition of knowledge. In a less elevated way, the next pages engage with a string of subjects that are connected by one aesthetic thread. If some object to the concision of part of these essays, I shall in my defense advocate Callimachus' preference for small and defined compositions. Of the poet of Cyrene, however, I hope to share not the polemic tone, but the playful note.

[1] An Italian version, with variants, of the first essay has been published as 'La filosofia come spunto poetico e polemico in Callimaco', in P.B. Cipolla (ed.), *Metodo e Passione. Atti dell'Incontro di Studi in onore di Giuseppina Basta Donzelli* (Catania, 11-12 aprile 2016), Amsterdam 2018, pp. 75-94. An Italian version, with variants, of the third essay has been published as 'Idomeneo e Paride di fronte ad Elena: un esempio di libertà morale in *Enn.* III 3 (48) 5, 41-43,' in M. Di Pasquale Barbanti and D. Iozzia (edd.), *Anima e libertà in Plotino. Atti del convegno di Catania, 29-30 gennaio 2009*, Catania 2009, pp. 137-157.

Callimachus on the Pleasure of Knowledge

Why should we be concerned with Callimachus in the context of the relationship between philosophy and artistic production? It must be said that Callimachus is one of the poets who more openly manifests and defends a specific way of understanding poetry, and therefore he has a place in the history of ancient aesthetics. In addition to that, as demonstrated by Benjamin Acosta-Hughes and Susan Stephens, the poet shows clear contacts with Plato's and Aristotle's writings, and in general he takes part in a debate that goes back to the positions of the two great philosophers, probably to criticize both. To this I would add that it is more than likely that Callimachus knew the Socratic school of Cyrene, his hometown. This could also be foreshadowed in a specific passage of his poem *Aitia*. My claim is that it is significant that Callimachus in this passage examines the validity of the auditory and cognitive experience in opposition to other forms of pleasures, namely the sensual ones. Morevover, he appears to be connected,[1] both as an author and as a critic, to the literary disputes between Hellenistic philosophers as well as writers, as we can learn from the fragmented writings of Philodemus of Gadara. These aesthetic quarrels have their roots, of course, again in Plato and Aristotle. For these reasons Callimachus deserves to be read in the light of the literary and philosophical controversies, even those of a later date, which reflect the intellectual milieu of the time. Our knowledge in this field, however, remains rather limited due to the very sparce evidence that we have of them.

---

[1] Cf. A.J. Romano, 'Callimachus and Contemporary Criticism,' in B. Acosta-Hughes, L. Lehnus, S. Stephens (edd.), *Brill's Companion to Callimachus*, Leiden 2011, pp. 309-328.

Callimachus' position on his poetry

Callimachus occupies a special role in the history of literary criticism, as he was the leading man of letters at the court of Ptolemy the Second Philadelphus and his powerful sister-wife Arsinoe II, and of Ptolemy the Third Euergetes and his wife Berenice, and worked at the Library of Alexandria. Unfortunately, for the reconstruction of his oeuvre, apart from the *Hymns* and the *Epigrams*, we have only fragments (although some of considerable extension) of two of his main poetic works, the *Aitia* and the *Hecale*, and of the *Iambi*, while his prose works are completely lost. Among these were the encyclopedic *Pinakes*, a sort of annotated catalogue of all the contents of the Library, in which it was possible to find more explicit information on the vast literary and philosophical knowledge of the poet. An indication of Callimachus' importance in the history of ancient literature and culture is the fact that he was the source of inspiration for the Latin *poetae novi*, particularly Catullus, who famously made a Latin version of Callimachus' *Coma Berenices*, and Horace, who is a key figure in the history of ancient literary criticism and aesthetics.

In the last two decades, research on Callimachus has increased considerably and, for example, we now have two large and comprehensive commentaries of the *Aitia*,[2] which integrate the historical edition by Rudolph Pfeiffer[3] with more recent discoveries of papyri, and translate the fragmented text into modern languages. Alongside these commentaries, many important studies have been published, including some which have fo-

[2] G. Massimilla (ed.), *Callimaco, 'Aitia': Libri Primo e Secondo*, Pisa 1996; Id. (ed.), *Callimaco, 'Aitia': Libri Terzo e Quarto*, Pisa/Roma 2010; A. Harder (ed.), *Callimachus, 'Aetia'*, Oxford 2012.

[3] Pfeiffer (ed.), *Callimachus, vol. I: Fragmenta*, Oxford 1949.

cused on the role of philosophical knowledge in Callimachus,[4] and in particular have highlighted the many points of contact between him and Plato, whose dialogues were for the poet a sort of reference point, although often in a critical way.

In order to understand Callimachus' idea of poetry, I would like to start from an epigram, where in an erotic context we find a programmatic statement on his art:

> Ἐχθαίρω τὸ ποίημα τὸ κυκλικόν, οὐδὲ κελεύθῳ [in a road that carries many people]
> χαίρω, τίς πολλοὺς ὧδε καὶ ὧδε φέρει·
> μισέω καὶ περίφοιτον ἐρώμενον, οὐδ' ἀπὸ κρήνης
> πίνω· σικχαίνω πάντα τὰ δημόσια.
> Λυσανίη, σὺ δὲ ναίχι καλὸς καλός—ἀλλὰ πρὶν εἰπεῖν
> τοῦτο σαφῶς, Ἠχώ φησί τις· 'ἄλλος ἔχει.'[5]
>
> I hate the poems in the Epic Cycle, I don't like highways
> that are heavily traveled, I despise
> a promiscuous lover, and I don't drink from public fountains:
> Everything public disgusts me. And yes, Lysanias,
> you are handsome as handsome, but before I can even say it,
> back comes the echo: "Some other man has him." (tr. Lombardo-Rayor)

The text is erotic but also ironic and playful, according to the overall tone of his epigrams: note, for example, that Callimachus expresses his dislike with four different verbs. The poet here declares his desire not to follow, unlike many of his contemporaries, the paths that are already well-trodden in poetry

---

[4] B. Acosta-Hughes, L. Lehnus and S. Stephens, *Brill's Companion to Callimachus*, Leiden 2011; Benjamin Acosta-Hughes and Susan Stephens, *Callimachus in Context*, Cambridge 2012.
[5] Callimachus, *Ep*. 28.

as in love. In his general poetic production this is expressed through eccentric and remote myths, and through use of obscure words and etiologies, in parallel to the erudite character of his studies as a scholar. The manifesto of his poetry is clearly expressed in the conclusion of the *Hymn to Apollo* and in the prologue of the *Aitia*. In both texts Callimachus defends a kind of poetry which is *leptòs*, light and refined, in contrast to the example of the traditional epic poetry and all its supporters. These, we have to imagine, are not simply other poets (as it was thought in the past), but rather literary critics, who established rules of judgment on the work of others.

In the *Hymn to Apollo*, Callimachus proclaimes his stance against the epic tradition and claims to aspire to a pure and precious way of making poetry:

> ὁ Φθόνος Ἀπόλλωνος ἐπ᾽ οὔατα λάθριος εἶπεν
> "οὐκ ἄγαμαι τὸν ἀοιδὸν ὃς οὐδ᾽ ὅσα πόντος ἀείδει."
> τὸν Φθόνον ὡπόλλων ποδί τ᾽ ἤλασεν ὧδέ τ᾽ ἔειπεν·
> "Ἀσσυρίου ποταμοῖο μέγας ῥόος, ἀλλὰ τὰ πολλὰ
> λύματα γῆς καὶ πολλὸν ἐφ᾽ ὕδατι συρφετὸν ἕλκει.
> Δηοῖ δ᾽ οὐκ ἀπὸ παντὸς ὕδωρ φορέουσι Μέλισσαι,
> ἀλλ᾽ ἥτις καθαρή τε καὶ ἀχράαντος ἀνέρπει
> πίδακος ἐξ ἱερῆς ὀλίγη λιβὰς ἄκρον ἄωτον."
> χαῖρε ἄναξ· ὁ δὲ Μῶμος, ἵν᾽ ὁ Φθόνος, ἔνθα νέοιτο.[6]
>
> Spake Envy privily in the ear of Apollo: "I
> admire not the poet who singeth not things for number as the sea."
> Apollo spurned Envy with his foot and spake thus:
> "Great is the stream of the Assyrian river, but much
> filth of earth and much refuse it carries on its waters.
> And not of every water do the Melissae carry to Deo,

[6] Callimachus, *Hymn to Apollo* 105-113.

> but of the trickling stream that springs from a holy fountain,
> pure and undefiled, the very crown of waters."
> Hail, O Lord, but Blame—let him go where Envy dwells! (tr. Mair)

Traditional epic poetry is likened to a vast river that carries with it all the debris and impurities, unlike a shorter poem which is pure and not polluted. Here we might also see a criticism of the Platonic position in the *Ion*, through the image of the bee: it seems that Callimachus agrees with the words of Socrates, but interprets the overall conceptions on the condition of the inspired poet of the *Ion* in a different way, as we will see.

The so-called prologue of the Telchines is found at the beginning of the *Aitia* but was probably composed in old age, although the reconstruction of the edition of the *Aitia* is not at all clear. In it, Callimachus attacks vehemently the Telchines, mythological creatures described as opponents of the Muses, who mumble at the poet because of his choice to compose only a short poem. It is not clear who Callimachus was writing against, although a list of the Telchines survives in a papyrus scholion where, alongside some epigrammatists, we can read the name of Praxiphanes. In general it seems clear that the reference is against those who, poets and above all critics, prefer epic poetry and do not understand the subtlety and, in a way, the modernity of Callimachus' poetry.

Although in the past it was thought that the Telchines represented poets such as Apollonius Rhodius insofar as they recovered styles and modes of the epic tradition, or even, in a joking tone, other poets active at the Ptolemaic court, such as Theocritus, now scholars believe that Callimachus alludes more to the *critics* than to the *makers* of poetry:

[…] Ἀ[πό]λλων εἶπεν ὅ μοι Λύκιος·
’.......]... ἀοιδέ, τὸ μὲν θύος ὅττι πάχιστον
  θρέψαι, τὴ]ν Μοῦσαν δ’ ὠγαθὲ λεπταλέην·
πρὸς δέ σε] καὶ τόδ’ ἄνωγα, τὰ μὴ πατέουσιν ἅμαξαι
  τὰ στείβειν, ἑτέρων ἴχνια μὴ καθ’ ὁμά
δίφρον ἐλ]ᾶν μηδ’ οἶμον ἀνὰ πλατύν, ἀλλὰ κελεύθους
  ἀτρίπτο]υς, εἰ καὶ στειν̣οτέρην ἐλάσεις.’
τῷ πιθόμη]ν· ἐνὶ τοῖς γὰρ ἀείδομεν οἳ λιγὺν ἦχον
  τέττιγος, θ]όρυβον δ’ οὐκ ἐφίλησαν ὄνων.
θηρὶ μὲν οὐατόεντι πανείκελον ὀγκήσαιτο
  ἄλλος, ἐγ]ὼ δ’ εἴην οὑλ̣[α]χύς, ὁ πτερόεις,
ἆ πάντως, ἵνα γῆρας ἵνα δρόσον ἣν μὲν ἀείδω
  πρώκιον ἐκ δίης ἠέρος εἶδαρ ἔδων,
αὖθι τὸ̣ δ’ ἐκδύοιμι, τό μοι βάρος ὅσσον ἔπεστι
  τριγλ̣ώχιν̣ ὀλοῷ νῆσος ἐπ’ Ἐγκελάδῳ.
.... Μοῦσαι γὰρ ὅσους ἴδον ὄθματι παῖδας
  μὴ λοξῷ, πολιοὺς οὐκ ἀπέθεντο φίλους.[7]

For when I put a writing-tablet on my knees for the first time
  Apollo Lycius [Laisius] said to me:
‘…poet, feed the sacrificial animal so that it becomes as fat
  as possible, but, my dear fellow, keep the Muse slender;
besides, I also urge you to go where big waggons never go,
  to drive your chariot not in the same tracks as others
and not along a wide road, but along untrodden paths,
  even if you will drive it along a more narrow one.’
I obeyed him; for we sing among those who love the clear sound
  of the cicada, but not the noise of the asses.
Let somebody else bray exactly like the long-eared animal,
  let me be the small one, the winged one,
oh, in all respects, in order that, as to old age and as to dew,
  I may sing like the second – eating the free food from the
divine sky – and throw off the first again, which weighs on me

[7] Callimachus, *Aitia* fr. 1. 22-38.

like the island with three points on the destructive Enceladus.
… for, whomsoever the Muses did not look at askance as a child
they will not reject as a friend when he is old. (tr. Harder)

The image of the cicada as a paradigm for the poet is particularly intriguing for us because it appears to be a specific reference to Plato's *Phaedrus*: here, in fact, Socrates recalls a myth about cicadas, who were originally men and have been transformed into insects to devote themselves entirely to the Muses:

Φαῖδρος
ἔχουσι δὲ δὴ τί τοῦτο; ἀνήκοος γάρ, ὡς ἔοικε, τυγχάνω ὤν.

Σωκράτης
οὐ μὲν δὴ πρέπει γε φιλόμουσον ἄνδρα τῶν τοιούτων ἀνήκοον εἶναι. λέγεται δ᾽ ὥς ποτ᾽ ἦσαν οὗτοι ἄνθρωποι τῶν πρὶν μούσας γεγονέναι, γενομένων δὲ Μουσῶν καὶ φανείσης ᾠδῆς οὕτως ἄρα τινὲς τῶν τότε ἐξεπλάγησαν ὑφ᾽ ἡδονῆς, [259c] ὥστε ᾄδοντες ἠμέλησαν σίτων τε καὶ ποτῶν, καὶ ἔλαθον τελευτήσαντες αὑτούς: ἐξ ὧν τὸ τεττίγων γένος μετ᾽ ἐκεῖνο φύεται, γέρας τοῦτο παρὰ Μουσῶν λαβόν, μηδὲν τροφῆς δεῖσθαι γενόμενον, ἀλλ᾽ ἄσιτόν τε καὶ ἄποτον εὐθὺς ᾄδειν, ἕως ἂν τελευτήσῃ, καὶ μετὰ ταῦτα ἐλθὸν παρὰ μούσας ἀπαγγέλλειν τίς τίνα αὐτῶν τιμᾷ τῶν ἐνθάδε. Τερψιχόρᾳ μὲν οὖν τοὺς ἐν τοῖς χοροῖς τετιμηκότας αὐτὴν ἀπαγγέλλοντες [259d] ποιοῦσι προσφιλεστέρους, τῇ δὲ Ἐρατοῖ τοὺς ἐν τοῖς ἐρωτικοῖς, καὶ ταῖς ἄλλαις οὕτως, κατὰ τὸ εἶδος ἑκάστης τιμῆς: τῇ δὲ πρεσβυτάτῃ Καλλιόπῃ καὶ τῇ μετ᾽ αὐτὴν Οὐρανίᾳ τοὺς ἐν φιλοσοφίᾳ διάγοντάς τε καὶ τιμῶντας τὴν ἐκείνων μουσικὴν ἀγγέλλουσιν, αἳ δὴ μάλιστα τῶν Μουσῶν περί τε οὐρανὸν καὶ λόγους οὖσαι θείους τε καὶ ἀνθρωπίνους ἱᾶσιν καλλίστην φωνήν.[8]

[8] Plato, *Phaedr*. 259b-259d.

> Phaedrus
>
> And what gift is that? This information seems to have passed me by.
>
> Socrates
>
> It's quite wrong for a devotee of the Muses not to have heard about this. It is said that these cicadas were once men, in the days before the Muses were born. When the Muses were born and singing had been invented, the story goes that some of the men of that time were ecstatic with pleasure, and were so busy singing that they didn't bother with food and drink, so that before they knew it they were dead. They were the origin of the race of cicadas, whom the Muses granted the gift of never needing any food once they were born; all they do is sing, from the moment of their births until their deaths, without eating or drinking. After dying they go to the Muses and tell them which men here on earth honoured which of them. They tell Terpsichore the names of those who have honoured her with dances and raise them higher in her favour; they tell Erato the names of those who have honoured her in the ways of love, and so on for all the other Muses, according to each one's area of responsibility. But they tell Calliope, the oldest of the Muses, and her companion Urania about those who spent their lives doing philosophy and honouring their particular kind of music. I should say that these two are the Muses who are especially concerned with the heavens and with the way both gods and men use words, and that there is no more beautiful sound than their voices. (tr. Waterfield)

It must be said that Callimachus may have not found the image of men as cicadas only in Plato, as it is already present in Homer, *Il.* 3, 151-2, and Archilochus fr. 223, but in employing this reference to Plato he seems to emphasize the independence of the poet at the very beginning of his main work. Also, the reference to the need to judge the poet according to his own *techne* seems directed to the Platonic critique of the figure of the poet as expressed in the *Ion*. At the same time, Callimachus appreciates the concept that poets are inspired by the Muses, but inteprets it in agreement with the poetic tradition and in opposition to Plato, as a recognition of his own validity as a poet. Finally, it is very clear from other texts that Callimachus refuses the very idea that a poet is competent only in one Muse, that is, only in one literary genre.[9]

Callimachus and philosophy

We must stress that the many references to Plato do not indicate that Callimachus adhered to the Platonic philosophy, but rather that he knew and read Plato's writings and discussed them, probably as a sign of broader disputes about the role of poetry. A specific evidence of his interest and also of his reaction to Plato is visible in the epigram 23,[10] which regards (probably with an ironic tone) the suicide of a young man who had read the *Phaedo*.

Εἴπας ῞῞Ηλιε χαῖρε῝ Κλεόμβροτος ὡμβρακιώτης
  ἧλατ῝ ἀφ῝ ὑψηλοῦ τείχεος εἰς Ἀΐδην,
ἄξιον οὐδὲν ἰδὼν θανάτου κακόν, ἀλλὰ Πλάτωνος
  ἓν τὸ περὶ ψυχῆς γράμμ῝ ἀναλεξάμενος.[11]

Kleombrotus of Ambrakia said "Farewell
    Sun," and leaped from a high wall clear into Hades.
Not that he had seen some evil that merited death,

---

[9] Cf. P. Murray, 'Poetic Inspiration,' in P. Murray and P. Destrée (edd.), *Blackwell Companion to Ancient Aesthetics*, Malden, MA 2015, p. 170.

[10] Cf. S.A. White, 'Callimachus on Plato and Cleombrotus,' in *Transactions of the American Philological Association* 124 (1994), pp. 135-161. White believes that Callimachus is a follower of Plato's philosophy. See also Tom Hawkins, *Iambic Poetics in the Roman Empire*, Cambridge 2014, pp. 55-58.

[11] Callimachus, *Ep*. 23.

> But he had just finished reading Plato's *On the soul.* (tr. Lombardo-Rayor, modified)

It is clear that the dialogue on the soul mentioned by Callimachus is the *Phaedo*, already known during antiquity under this name. Moreover, a certain Cleombrotus is mentioned in the dialogue, along with Aristippus of Cyrene, among the disciples of Socrates who were not present at his death, although it is not clear if this is the same Cleombrotus that Callimachus is talking about. We may think that this is a literary game on Callimachus' part, which highlights the ambiguities of a superficial reading of Plato, in the sense that Cleombrotus was not present at Socrates' death and would not have understood that the philosopher didn't encourage suicide.[12] The epigram might even criticize Plato himself, although it seems that it is rather a superficial reading of his dialogues that Callimachus wants to condemn. Indeed, the very problem of a bad influence of philosophy on the young affected the school of Cyrene, where Hegesias was regarded as an instigator of death (besides perhaps be aware of Buddhism). An example of this is a passage from Cicero that is precisely an important testimony of Hegesias and connects directly Callimachus' epigram to the issue of Hegesias' version of the Cyrenaic teachings.

> A malis igitur mors abducit, non a bonis, verum si quaerimus. et quidem hoc a Cyrenaico Hegesia sic copiose disputatur, ut is a rege Ptolomaeo prohibitus esse dicatur illa in scholis dicere, quod multi is auditis mortem sibi ipsi consciscerent. [84] Callimachi quidem epigramma in Ambraciotam Theombrotum[13] est, quem ait, cum ei nihil accidisset adversi, e muro se in mare abiecisse

[12] Cf. Plato, *Phaed.* 61c-62c.

[13] *Sic* in Cicero's text: cf. G. D. Williams, 'Cleombrotus of Ambracia: Interpretations of a Suicide from Callimachus to Agathias', in *Classical Quarterly* 45 (1995), pp. 154-169.

> lecto Platonis libro. eius autem, quem dixi, Hegesiae liber est Ἀποκαρτερῶν, quo a vita quidem per inediam discedens revocatur ab amicis; quibus respondens vitae humanae enumerat incommoda. possem idem facere, etsi minus quam ille, qui omnino vivere expedire nemini putat. mitto alios: etiamne nobis expedit? qui et domesticis et forensibus solaciis ornamentisque privati certe si ante occidissemus, mors nos a malis, non a bonis abstraxisset.[14]
>
> Death then withdraws us from evil, not from good, if truth is our object. Indeed this thought is discussed by Hegesias the Cyrenaic with such wealth of illustration that the story goes that he was stopped from lecturing on the subject by King Ptolemy, because a number of his listeners afterwards committed suicide. There is an epigram of Callimachus upon Cleombrotus of Ambracia who, he says, without having met with any misfortune, flung himself from the city wall into the sea after reading Plato's book. Now in the book of Hegesias whom I have mentioned,'Αποκαρτερῶν [*a man who starves himself*], there appears a man who was passing away from life by starvation and is called back by his friends, and in answer to their remònstrances, details the discomforts of human life. I could do the same, but I should not go so far as he does in thinking it no advantage at all for anyone to live. Other cases I wave aside: is it an advantage still to me? I have been robbed of the consolations of family life and the distinctions of a public career, and assuredly, if we had died before this happened, death would have snatched us from evil, not from good. (tr. King)

Here we will not deal with the question whether Cicero is a reliable source (he mentions, probably from memory, a Theombrotus instead of Cleombrotus). But it is significant that Callimachus' epigram is used as an example of the dangers of philosophy. Plato in fact is openly recognized by Callimachus

[14] Cicero, *Tusculanae Disputationae* 1.34.83-84.

as a philosophical point of reference and the poet is a witness of the fact that the Platonic philosophy had a specific presence in the Alexandrian culture of the third century.

Of the greatest interest for this subject is Callimachus' literary quarrel with Plato in the unfortunately extremely fragmented *Iambus* 13, where the poet defends his ability to write in different genres, as Ion of Chios had done before him. The iambus is extremely fragmented and I quote only a few lines, some unfortunately with no clear connections to the others.

> […]
> Ἰαστὶ καὶ Δωριστὶ καὶ τὸ σύμμικ|τ̣ο̣ν[(18)
> […]
> σὺ πεντάμετρα συντίθει, σὺ δ̣' η̣[ρῷ̣ο]ν,
> σὺ δὲ τραγῳ̣δ̣ε̣[ῖν] ἐκ θεῶν ἐκληρώσω̣ ;
> δοκέω μὲν οὐδείς, ἀλλὰ καὶ το.δ..κεψαι . . . . . . (33)[15]

> […] Ionic and Doric and a mixture of both. […] (who said) "Do you compose pentameters and you epics; the gods have allotted that you write tragedies"? Nobody, I believe, but . . . (tr. Trypanis)

This is a central affirmation within Callimachus' poetic, one which is in open opposition to the Platonic view expressed in the *Ion* (and, as we have seen, in the *Phaedrus* as well). According to Susan Stephens, in this *Iambus* we should retrieve an allusion to the Platonic dialogue in the very use of the name Ion, here of course referred to the poet from Chios while Plato's rapsod is from Ephesus, a city which is also mentioned, in relation to Hipponax, at the end of the poem. This theory may not be fully convincing, however it is not unlikely

[15] Callimachus, *Iambus* 13, 18-33.

if we consider the subtle and complex web of literary games in Callimachus' poetry. Nevertheless it seems quite clear that Plato's view on poets is one of the specific polemical targets of Callimachus, as we can see also in the prologue of the *Aitia*. In the *Ion*, in fact, Socrates declares the impossibility for the rapsod to be excellent in more than one kind of poetry:

> ἅτε οὖν οὐ τέχνῃ ποιοῦντες καὶ πολλὰ λέγοντες καὶ καλὰ περὶ [534c] τῶν πραγμάτων, ὥσπερ σὺ περὶ Ὁμήρου, ἀλλὰ θείᾳ μοίρᾳ, τοῦτο μόνον οἷός τε ἕκαστος ποιεῖν καλῶς ἐφ' ὃ ἡ Μοῦσα αὐτὸν ὥρμησεν, ὁ μὲν διθυράμβους, ὁ δὲ ἐγκώμια, ὁ δὲ ὑπορχήματα, ὁ δ' ἔπη, ὁ δ' ἰάμβους: τὰ δ' ἄλλα φαῦλος αὐτῶν ἕκαστός ἐστιν. οὐ γὰρ τέχνῃ ταῦτα λέγουσιν ἀλλὰ θείᾳ δυνάμει, ἐπεί, εἰ περὶ ἑνὸς τέχνῃ καλῶς ἠπίσταντο λέγειν, κἂν περὶ τῶν ἄλλων ἁπάντων. διὰ ταῦτα δὲ ὁ θεὸς ἐξαιρούμενος τούτων τὸν νοῦν τούτοις χρῆται ὑπηρέταις καὶ [534d] τοῖς χρησμῳδοῖς καὶ τοῖς μάντεσι τοῖς θείοις, ἵνα ἡμεῖς οἱ ἀκούοντες εἰδῶμεν ὅτι οὐχ οὗτοί εἰσιν οἱ ταῦτα λέγοντες οὕτω πολλοῦ ἄξια, οἷς νοῦς μὴ πάρεστιν, ἀλλ' ὁ θεὸς αὐτός ἐστιν ὁ λέγων, διὰ τούτων δὲ φθέγγεται πρὸς ἡμᾶς. μέγιστον δὲ τεκμήριον τῷ λόγῳ Τύννιχος ὁ Χαλκιδεύς, ὃς ἄλλο μὲν οὐδὲν πώποτε ἐποίησε ποίημα ὅτου τις ἂν ἀξιώσειεν μνησθῆναι, τὸν δὲ παίωνα ὃν πάντες ᾄδουσι, σχεδόν τι πάντων μελῶν κάλλιστον, ἀτεχνῶς, ὅπερ αὐτὸς λέγει, [534e] 'εὕρημά τι Μοισᾶν.' ἐν τούτῳ γὰρ δὴ μάλιστά μοι δοκεῖ ὁ θεὸς ἐνδείξασθαι ἡμῖν, ἵνα μὴ διστάζωμεν, ὅτι οὐκ ἀνθρώπινά ἐστιν τὰ καλὰ ταῦτα ποιήματα οὐδὲ ἀνθρώπων, ἀλλὰ θεῖα καὶ θεῶν, οἱ δὲ ποιηταὶ οὐδὲν ἀλλ' ἢ ἑρμηνῆς εἰσιν τῶν θεῶν, κατεχόμενοι ἐξ ὅτου ἂν ἕκαστος κατέχηται. ταῦτα ἐνδεικνύμενος ὁ θεὸς ἐξεπίτηδες διὰ τοῦ φαυλοτάτου [535a] ποιητοῦ τὸ κάλλιστον μέλος ᾖσεν.[16]

So each poet can compose fine poems only in the genre to which the Muse has urged him – one dithyrambs, another encomia, another dance-songs, another epic, another poems in iambics. Each

[16] Plato, *Ion* 534b-435a.

> of them is bad at all the other genres. This is because it is by divine dispensation, not by skill, that they compose and utter many fine things about the world, just as you do about Homer. They do this not by skill but through a divine force, since, if it were by skill that they knew how to speak well about one subject, they would also know how to do so about all other subjects. That is why the god takes away these people's reason and uses them as ministers and givers of oracles and divine prophets so that we, who hear them, may know that it is not these people, whose reason is not in them, who are saying these things which are so valuable; rather the god himself is the speaker and is addressing us through them. The best evidence for what I am saying is Tynnichus of Chalcis who never composed any poem worth mentioning, other than the paean which everyone sings. This is almost the finest of all poems and, as he himself says, simply 'an invention of the Muses'. For in this way the god seems to me to show us, most clearly, so that we are in no doubt, that these fine poems are not human, nor produced by human beings, but are divine and produced by gods, and the poets are nothing but interpreters of the gods, each one possessed by the appropriate deity. As a way of showing this, the god deliberately sang the finest song through the worst poet. (tr. Sheppard)

Callimachus' reference to the *Ion*, however, is not limited to the *Iambus* 13, since we can detect it also in the closing of the *Hymn to Apollo*, where the poet openly declares that his role is to tap into pure water like bees. Although here the poet probably refers to the priestesses of Demeter, who were called *Melissai*, it seems that he is also alluding to a similar description of the poets' activity which can be found in the *Ion*, however with a different meaning (the very one that Callimachus intends to challenge):

> ὥσπερ αἱ βάκχαι ἀρύονται ἐκ τῶν ποταμῶν μέλι καὶ γάλα κατεχόμεναι, ἔμφρονες δὲ οὖσαι οὔ, καὶ τῶν μελοποιῶν ἡ ψυχὴ

> τοῦτο ἐργάζεται, ὅπερ αὐτοὶ λέγουσι. λέγουσι γὰρ δήπουθεν πρὸς ἡμᾶς οἱ ποιηταὶ ὅτι [534b] ἀπὸ κρηνῶν μελιρρύτων ἐκ Μουσῶν κήπων τινῶν καὶ ναπῶν δρεπόμενοι τὰ μέλη ἡμῖν φέρουσιν ὥσπερ αἱ μέλιτται, καὶ αὐτοὶ οὕτω πετόμενοι: καὶ ἀληθῆ λέγουσι. κοῦφον γὰρ χρῆμα ποιητής ἐστιν καὶ πτηνὸν καὶ ἱερόν, καὶ οὐ πρότερον οἷός τε ποιεῖν πρὶν ἂν ἔνθεός τε γένηται καὶ ἔκφρων καὶ ὁ νοῦς μηκέτι ἐν αὐτῷ ἐνῇ: ἕως δ' ἂν τουτὶ ἔχῃ τὸ κτῆμα, ἀδύνατος πᾶς ποιεῖν ἄνθρωπός ἐστιν καὶ χρησμῳδεῖν.[17]
>
> Just as Bacchants, when possessed, draw honey and milk from rivers and are not in their right minds, so the lyric poets' soul does this too, as they themselves say. To be sure the poets tell us that they bring us their poems like bees, gathering them from springs flowing with honey in groves and gardens of the Muses, and they claim that they are winged, like bees; and they tell the truth. For a poet is a light, winged, holy thing, unable to compose until he is inspired and out of his mind, his reason no longer in him; no one can compose poetry or give oracles as long as they have their reason. (tr. Sheppard)

Finally, with regard to Callimachus' criticism on Plato, we should consider a passage from Proclus' commentary on the *Timaeus*, which claims that Callimachus did not consider Plato as a competent critic of poetry.[18] Unfortunately we do not know which Callimachean texts Proclus was referring to, but it was probably one of the prose works:

---

[17] Plato, *Ion* 534a-b.

[18] On Proclus' poetics, see A. Sheppard, *Studies on the 5th and 6th Essays of Proclus' Commentary on the 'Republic'*, Göttingen 1980; and also R.L. Cardullo, *Il linguaggio del simbolo in Proclo: analisi filosofico-semantica dei termini symbolon/eikôn/synthêma nel 'Commentario alla Repubblica'*, Catania 1985.

> εἴπερ γάρ τις ἄλλος καὶ ποιητῶν ἄριστος κριτὴς ὁ Πλάτων, ὡς καὶ Λογγῖνος συνίστησιν. Ἡρακλείδης γοῦν ὁ Ποντικός φησιν, ὅτι τῶν Χοιρίλου τότε εὐδοκιμούντων Πλάτων τὰ Ἀντιμάχου προὐτίμησε καὶ αὐτὸν ἔπεισε τὸν Ἡρακλείδην εἰς Κολοφῶνα ἐλθόντα τὰ ποιήματα συλλέξαι τοῦ ἀνδρός. μάτην οὖν φληναφῶσι Καλλίμαχος καὶ Δοῦρις ὡς Πλάτωνος οὐκ ὄντος ἱκανοῦ κρίνειν ποιητάς·[19]

> For Plato was as excellent a critic of poets as anyone, as also Longinus proves. For Heracleides Ponticus says that, of the poets famous at the time of Choerilus, Plato preferred Antimachus, and he persuaded Heracleides, when he was going to Colophon, to collect Antimachus' poems. Callimachus and Duris speak non-sense when they say that Plato was not competent to judge poets. (tr. Acosta-Hughes)

In general, we can certainly say that Plato is a 'central and significant intertext within Callimachus' poetic heritage'.[20] The prologue of the *Aitia*, in the words of Penelope Murray, is a 'complex act of artistic self-definition in which Callimachus seeks to reclaim for poetry the cultural authority that it once had by restoring the earlier relationship between inspiration, *techne*, and *sophia*, which Plato had blown apart.'[21]

Besides Plato, however, we can detect also a strong Aristotelian tone in the titles of Callimachus' prose writings. The ancient sources attribute to Callimachus almost eight hundred works, although this is probably an incorrect number. The titles of some of them, all sadly lost, (for example *On birds*, *On fish*, *On winds*, *Marvels throughout the world by location*)

---

[19] Proclus, *In Timaeum* 1.90.26.
[20] B. Acosta-Hughes and S. Stephens, *Callimachus in context*, cit., p. 82.
[21] P. Murray, 'Poetic Inspiration,' in P. Murray and P. Destrée (edd.), *Blackwell Companion to Ancient Aesthetics*, cit., p. 170.

seem to be connected to Aristotle's structure of sciences, and some scholars in the past have conjectured that the young Callimachus frequented the *Peripatos* during a supposed stay in Athens. This assumption is now obsolete due to the lack of sufficient documentary support, however the Aristotelian flavour of his prose titles, which cannot be denied, may be due to the presence in Alexandria of Demetrius Phalereus, who had been a pupil of Theophrastus and had a role in organizing the *Mouseion* following Peripatetic criteria. Therefore Callimachus himself, as one of the main scholars of the library, would have adhered to the principles of Aristotelian research.[22]

One element that traditionally had led to the supposition that Callimachus embraced Aristotelianism is the title of a lost work, *Pros Praxiphanes*, understood as 'in defense of Praxiphanes,' who was the successor of Theophrastus. Praxiphanes wrote, among other things, two works of poetic criticism, *On Poems* and *On Poets*, of which, again, we do not know much. The Florentine Scholia to the prologue of the *Aitia*, however, overturned this interpretation, revealing that Praxiphanes was one of the Telchines with which Callimachus, as we have seen, strongly argued. Therefore the title is now interpreted as *Against Praxiphanes* and therefore against the Peripatetic positions on the need for unity in poetry as opposed to history, a conception that Callimachus clearly rejects. Unfortunately not much more can be said about the details of his dispute against Peripatetic literary criticism. In general, though, it can be said

---

[22] For example, in the *Epigram* 5 he describes a nautilus following Aristotle, *Historia Animalium* 622b5-15: cf. K. Gutzwiller, 'The Nautilus, the Halcyon, and Selenaia: Callimachus's *Epigram* 5 Pf. = 14 G. – P,' in *Classical Antiquity* 11, 1992, pp. 194-209.

that Callimachus deliberately puts himself at the centre of the literary discussions of the Hellenistic period.

In my opinion we can certainly admit that if, on the one hand, Callimachus' philological and erudite attitude is fully in agreement with the Peripatetic research lines, on the other hand it is equally true that Callimachus, in claiming his own creative independence, can well have as one of his polemical targets the critical restrictions caused by Aristotle's views on poetry. If it is true that Plato's texts are present in the work of Callimachus and that, as evidenced by *Iambus* 13, Plato is criticized, albeit indirectly, for his views on the role of poets in the *Ion*, even stronger is Callimachus' dissatisfaction or even intolerance towards poetic precepts that we can identify as vaguely Peripatetic, although later they will be reprised by some Stoics. Callimachus therefore, while accepting the scientific and philological approach of Aristotle's school,[23] rejects any attempt to rule poetry from the outside, through the lens of the literary critic and not of the maker.

Pleasure and knowledge in Aitia *43*

Having in mind the cultural horizon in which Callimachus works, I would like now to move to the fragment 43 from the second book of the *Aitia*. For our perception of ancient literature it remains a paradox to say that 'it is hardly too much of an exaggeration that the *Aitia* is second in historical import-

[23] Cf. K. O. Brink, 'Callimachus and Aristotle: An Inquiry into Callimachus' ΠΡΟΣ ΠΡΑΞΙΦΑΝΗΝ', in *Classical Quarterly*, 40 (1946), p. 18.

ance only to the Homeric poems,'[24] as A.W. Bullock stated, and it is well known that the reason for the common disaffection with the poet of Cyrene, and to his etiologic poem in particular, derives not from the fact that (largely thanks to the discovery of papyri) we can read just a few fragments, but because of the highly scholarly and artful nature of his poetry. Despite the fact that the discovery of the papyri and their magisterial edition by Rudolph Pfeiffer have enabled us to know a wider section of Callimachus' writings than before, the common view on the poetry of the poet-philologist is still that of a perverted result of the classical tradition. Nevertheless it is also true that the very challenge posed by the reconstruction of the papyri has caused the growing interest of scholars.

Putting aside aesthetic considerations on his work, we can focus on a passage that was already known from indirect tradition and which presents, in poetic language, a reflection on the duration of pleasure that does not seem alien to the considerations on the same subject by some philosophical currents at the time of Callimachus or shortly before. It was Stobaeus who preserved the three elegiac couplets, affirming that they belong to the second book of the *Aitia*. The discovery of Callimachus' papyri, although dramatically mutilated, made it possible to confirm Stobaeus' indication and to place the six verses precisely almost at the beginning of the second book. Their context is the Muse's narration of a number of myths concerning the founding of cities in Sicily and for this reason, since the publication of the papyri, scholarly attention has understandably focused on the historical and indeed etiological information provided by Callimachus. However, it is un-

---

[24] A.W. Bulloch, 'Hellenistic Poetry,' in *The Cambridge History of Classical Literature* (ed. by P.E. Easterling, E.J. Kenney, B.M.W. Knox, M.V. Clausen) *I: Greek Literature*, Cambridge 1985, p. 553.

deniable that to focus only on the erudite details can cause us to miss the primary sense of Callimachus' poetry, which is to delight through learning. These verses in fact are an example of Callimachus' attitude towards his art and knowledge in general:

καὶ γὰρ ἐγὼ τὰ μὲν ὅσσα καρήατι τῆμος ἔδωκα
ξαἰνθὰ σὺν εὐόδμοις ἁβρὰ λίπη στεφάνοις,
ἄπνοἰα πάντ' ἐγένοντο παρὰ χρέος, ὅσσα τ' ὀδόντων
ἔνδοἰθι νείαιράν τ' εἰς ἀχάριστον ἔδυ,
καὶ τῶν ἰοὐδὲν ἔμεινεν ἐς αὔριον· ὅσσα δ' ἀκουαῖς
εἰσεθέἰμην, ἔτι μοι μοῦνα πάρεστι τάδε.[25]

For in my case too, everything I put on my head in that occasion,
the soft golden oil with fragrant wreaths,
immediately faded and died, and everything that went
into my mouth and down into my ungrateful belly,
of those things too nothing remained until the morning; but everything I
admitted to my ears, that only is still with me. (tr. Harder)

Despite some conjectures that connect the fr. 43 to fr. 178 (which describes the banquet at the Athenian Pollis' house), nothing can be said with certainty about the wider context in which the fragment is located. It is clear that the verses allude to a symposium and it is more than likely that here the poet speaks in the first person, but there is no reason to exclude the possibility that Callimachus used more than once the device of a banquet within the poem, for example for reasons of symmetry. Nothing can therefore be inferred from the previous verses, of which few letters remain, but it must be assumed that the poet had learned something (or even, if we consider what follows in the fragment, a large number of myths). It is

[25] Callimachus, *Aitia* fr. 43.12-17.

only in vv. 45-92 of the fragment that we can read an almost complete text which is, even with limitations, intelligible. In general the fragment 43 is of great importance because of its extension, which allows us to understand the narratological technique of Callimachus, which had wowed his Latin imitators. These verses are also a very clear example of Callimachus' ardous elocution, requiring some effort to be reconstituted and interpreted.

The meaning of the verses, developed according to the form of the *priamel*, is evident and it was understood as moralizing in scope: that is, physical pleasures pass, while knowledge remains. This reading, however, might not grasp an implicit aspect in the text, which is that learning itself produces a sort of pleasure, a concept that is similar to some positions of the Hellenistic schools. In a sort of *vanitas* in poetry, Callimachus describes the inanity of the material pleasures of the banquet: the perception of the perfumes fades with more immediacy, while the satisfaction of the belly lasts only a little bit longer. What he has learned through hearing, however, remains. Although the following verses are almost entirely missing, it is evident that the poet through the technique of paratactic comparison presents a scale of values, within which knowledge surpasses physical pleasures. It seems noteworthy to point out that scents and food as well as intellectual notions are considered as external objects physically entering the participant at the banquet: in fact, with brutal frankness (possibly derived from the iambic style), food is introduced through the mouth into the stomach, from which it disappears in a few hours, in the same way that the information given during the banquet is absorbed through the ears, to be preserved in this case indefinitely.

Learning itself seems to be considered implicitly as one of the symposiastic pleasures, however subtle and elevated, because of the comparison with the other two forms of pleasure. The erudite activities of the poet, after all, whose extension is surprising, could arise from the actual pleasure in the discovery of long lost information and in the identification of links between names, cults and places, which can be seen everywhere in his works and in the titles of the lost writings.

The most recent commentaries correctly compare Callimachus' passage to the epitaph of Sardanapalus (the debauched Assyrian king) attributed to Choerilus:

> εὖ εἰδὼς ὅτι θνητὸς ἔφυς σὸν θυμὸν ἄεξε
> τερπόμενος θαλίῃσι· θανόντι τοι οὔτις ὄνησις.
> καὶ γὰρ ἐγὼ σποδός εἰμι, Νίνου μεγάλης βασιλεύσας.
> ταῦτ' ἔχω ὅσσ' ἔφαγον καὶ ἐφύβρισα καὶ μετ' ἔρωτος
> τέρπν' ἔπαθον· τὰ δὲ πολλὰ καὶ ὄλβια κεῖνα λέλειπται.
> {ἥδε σοφὴ βιότοιο παραίνεσις, οὐδέ ποτ' αὐτῆς
> λήσομαι· ἐκτήσθω δ' ὁ θέλων τὸν ἀπείρονα χρυσόν.}[26]

> Though knowing full well that thou art but mortal, indulge thy desire, find joy in thy feasts. Dead, thou shalt have no delight. Yes, I am dust, though I was king of mighty Nineveh. *These are the things that I own, what I have eaten, what wantonness I have committed, what joys I received through passion; but my many rich possessions are now utterly dissolved.* This is a wise counsel for living, and I shall forget it never. Let him who wants it, acquire gold without end. (tr. Burton Gulick, modified)

We must also read, more significantly, the parodies of the epitaph by Crates of Thebes and Crysippus:

[26] Choerilus, fr. 335 SH [epitaph of Sardanapalus].

ταῦτ’ ἔχω, ὅσσ’ ἔμαθον καὶ ἐφρόντισα καὶ μετὰ Μουσῶν
σέμν’ ἐδάην· τὰ δὲ πολλὰ καὶ ὄλβια τῦφος ἔμαρψε.[27]

These are the things that I own, what I have learned and thought, and the Muses’
Solemn precepts; but all my riches delusion has seized. (tr. Hard, modified)

εὖ εἰδὼς ὅτι θνητὸς ἔφυς σὸν θυμὸν ἄεξε,
τερπόμενος μύθοισι· φαγόντι σοι οὔτις ὄνησις.
καὶ γὰρ ἐγὼ ῥάκος εἰμί, φαγὼν ὡς πλεῖστα καὶ ἡσθείς.
ταῦτ’ ἔχω ὅσσ’ ἔμαθον καὶ ἐφρόντισα καὶ μετὰ τούτων
ἔσθλ’ ἔπαθον· τὰ δὲ λοιπὰ καὶ ἡδέα πάντα λέλειπται.[28]

Keep in mind that you are mortal, and make yourself happy
by taking pleasure in conversation; nothing is any use to you after you eat it.
For I am a tattered bit of nothing, even though I ate and enjoyed myself as much as I could.
These are the things that I own, what I learned and thought, and the excellent
experiences that came with this, whereas everything else, pleasant though it all was, has perished. (tr. Olson, modified)

Callimachus therefore certainly fits into a tradition on the validity of the knowledge acquired at a banquet (for which we have also an example in Plato’s *Symposium*) and on the lack of importance of material pleasures, but at the same time his verses seem to highlight a topic which in the Hellenistic period becomes the subject of philosophical debate. Now, if this interpretation is plausible, it would lead to some conceptions of pleasure that developed within philosophical schools and which had been introduced by Aristippus. The fact that the

[27] Crates Cyn., fr. 355 SH.
[28] Chrysipp. Stoic., fr. 338 SH.

disciple of Socrates and his successors were from Cyrene, like Callimachus, might suggest at least that the poet was aware of Aristippus' teachings and of his school. As a result, many scholars believe that Callimachus had at least some notions of their philosophical doctrines, and Adelmo Barigazzi, for example, recognizes an echo of this in the verses of fragment 43.

In the case of Callimachus' verses, the consideration of different types of pleasure and their duration, despite the absence of clear indications, may be connected in some way to the philosophical reflections of the Cyrenaics and then of Epicurus. What I propose here is only a hypothesis derived from the observation of the text and from the fact that it is not unthinkable that Callimachus was aware of certain doctrines of the only school of philosophy of his hometown. If we accept this connection as a hypothesis, it does not mean that Callimachus had embraced the Cyrenaic doctrine of pleasure, which here might be actually rejected. This is simply a possible reading of the verses of the poet, who might well have known of the School of Cyrene and possibly of the debate on pleasure between this school and the Epicurean one. In general his preference for the enjoyment in learning is coherent with an Aristotelian point of view.

A final element to consider, in order to understand the extent of Callimachus' philosophical knowledge, is that it is possible that he was connected to the skeptic Timon of Phlius[29] and that he cites the works of Evemerus of Messene in the *Iamb* 1. Evemerus is sometimes included in same skeptic-atheist tradition as some Cyrenaics, which is another hint on the kind of

[29] Cf. Dee L. Clayman, *Timon of Phlius: Pyrrhonism into Poetry*, Berlin-New York 2009, pp. 147-157.

knowledge of philosophical thought that Callimachus had. It is notoriously extremely difficult to reconstruct the doctrines of the Cyrenaics.[30] One of the elements in the evolution of the school is the dialectic between pleasure and happiness, which sees Hegesias as an exponent of a pessimistic attitude, possibly because of a Cynical inspiration. For the Cyrenaics 'happiness, like those subjects and objects that populate it, is best described as the imperfect collection of transient episodes of pleasure […]. The importance of happiness could be derived only by linking all the episodes of past, present and future pleasures that the Cyrenaic individual happens to have experienced in their life […]; although remaining full hedonists, the Cyrenaics are not indifferent to happiness.'[31]

In the Hellenistic period the positions of the Cyrenaics were overcome by the Epicureans who consider pleasure differently and indentify it as absence of pain. Here certainly I do not mean to argue that Callimachus embraced a Epicurean theory, if in the verses of fr. 43 he had in mind the Cyrenaics to criticize them, but only that his position seems to be connected to a philosophical question about pleasure that was ever present in the Hellenistic thought. However, it must also be said that it is not entirely clear that the Cyrenaics were simply in favour of sensible pleasure,[32] because Annicerides reintroduced some civic values such as patriotism among the sources of pleasure, while Theodorus the Atheist declared that *sophro-*

---

[30] See K. Lampe, *The Birth of Hedonism: The Cyrenaic Philosophers and Pleasure as a Way of Life*, Princeton University Press, 2015.

[31] U. Zilioli, *The Cyrenaics*, Routledge 2012, p. 164.

[32] On the philosophical disputes on pleasure in the Hellenistic age, see V. Tsouna, 'Cyrenaics and Epicureans on Pleasure and the Good Life: The Original Debate and Its Later Revivals,' in S. Weisser and N. Thaler (edd.), *Strategies of Polemics in Greek and Roman Philosophy*, Leiden 2016, pp. 113-149.

syne (together with justice) was the foundation of happiness, which is the 'supreme desiderable,' in a way that resembles the Epicurean position, such as expressed by Epicurus himself in his *Letter to Menoeceus*:

> ὅταν οὖν λέγωμεν ἡδονὴν τέλος ὑπάρχειν, οὐ τὰς τῶν ἀσώτων ἡδονὰς καὶ τὰς ἐν ἀπολαύσει κειμένας λέγομεν, ὥς τινες ἀγνοοῦντες καὶ οὐχ ὁμολογοῦντες ἤ κακῶς ἐκδεχόμενοι νομίζουσιν, ἀλλὰ τὸ μήτε ἀλγεῖν κατὰ σῶμα μήτε ταράττεσθαι κατὰ ψυχήν. [132] οὐ γὰρ πότοι καὶ κῶμοι συνείροντες οὐδ' ἀπολαύσεις παίδων καὶ γυναικῶν οὐδ' ἰχθύων καὶ τῶν ἄλλων ὅσα φέρει πολυτελὴς τράπεζα, τὸν ἡδὺν γεννᾷ βίον, ἀλλὰ νήφων λογισμὸς καὶ τὰς αἰτίας ἐξερευνῶν πάσης αἱρέσεως καὶ φυγῆς καὶ τὰς δόξας ἐξελαύνων, ἐξ ὧν πλεῖστος τὰς ψυχὰς καταλαμβάνει θόρυβος. τούτων δὲ πάντων ἀρχὴ καὶ τὸ μέγιστον ἀγαθὸν φρόνησις. διὸ καὶ φιλοσοφίας τιμιώτερον ὑπάρχει φρόνησις, ἐξ ἧς αἱ λοιπαὶ πᾶσαι πεφύκασιν ἀρεταί.[33]
>
> So when we say that pleasure is the end, we do not mean the pleasures of the dissipated and those that consist in having a good time, as some out of ignorance and disagreement or refusal to understand suppose we do, but freedom from pain in the body and from disturbance in the soul. For what produces the pleasant life is not continuous drinking and parties or pederasty or womanizing or the enjoyment of fish and the other dishes of an expensive table, but sober reasoning which tracks down the causes of every choice and avoidance, and which banishes the opinions that beset souls with the greatest confusion. Of all this the beginning and the greatest good is prudence. Therefore prudence is even more precious than philosophy, and it is the natural source of all the remaining virtues. (tr. Long-Sedley)

It seems particularly useful here to highlight that Theodorus lived for some time in Alexandria, where he could have met

---

[33] Epicurus, *Ep. Men.* 131-132.

Callimachus, his fellow citizen. Moreover, according to some reconstructions, it is possible that the two were related.[34] Therefore, the verses of the fragment 43 may find a clearer identity as poetic interpretation of philosophical discussions which is more than likely that Callimachus knew. In general, I would add, the irreverent tone of individuality and self-expression in Callimachus has a common character with certain expressions of the Cyrenaic School, although we cannot infer from this that Callimachus embraced its philosophy. Theodorus and Evemerus, perhaps along with Timon of Phlius, appear to share the same irreverent attitude towards traditional conventions as, at the poetic level, Callimachus. Even Callimachus' choice of Plato as intertext, often in a veiled polemic, might have to do with knowledge of the teachings of the Cyrenaics and their position not certainly favourable to Plato.

In the context of the philosophical disputes between Hellenistic schools, I would like to mention an interesting text with respect to the issue of intellectual pleasure, in this case connected to artistic imitation, a passage from Plutarch's *Convivial Questions*, or *Table Talk*, which refers to a critique that the Cyrenaic school opposed to the Epicurean doctrine on pleasure.

> καὶ γὰρ ἐπὶ τῶν θεαμάτων ὅμοια πεπόνθαμεν ἀνθρώπους μὲν γὰρ ἀποθνήσκοντας. καὶ νοσοῦντας ἀνιαρῶς ὁρῶμεν: τὸν δὲ γεγραμμένον Φιλοκτήτην καὶ τὴν πεπλασμένην Ἰοκάστην, ἧς φασιν εἰς τὸ πρόσωπον ἀργύρου τι συμμῖξαι τὸν τεχνίτην, ὅπως ἐκλείποντος ἀνθρώπου καὶ μαραινομένου λάβῃ περιφάνειαν ὁ χαλκός, ἡδόμεθα καὶ θαυμάζομεν. 'τοῦτο δ'' εἶπον 'ἄνδρες Ἐπικούρειοι, καὶ τεκμήριόν ἐστι μέγα τοῖς Κυρηναϊκοῖς πρὸς

---

[34] Cf. C. Meillier, *Callimaque et son temp*, Alexandria 1979, pp. 335-337.

> ὑμᾶς τοῦ μὴ περὶ τὴν ὄψιν εἶναι μηδὲ περὶ τὴν ἀκοὴν ἀλλὰ περὶ τὴν διάνοιαν ἡμῶν τὸ ἡδόμενον ἐπὶ τοῖς ἀκούσμασι καὶ θεάμασιν. ἀλεκτορὶς γὰρ βοῶσα συνεχῶς καὶ κορώνη λυπηρὸν ἄκουσμα καὶ ἀηδές ἐστιν, ὁ δὲ μιμούμενος ἀλεκτορίδα βοῶσαν καὶ κορώνην εὐφραίνει. καὶ φθισικοὺς μὲν ὁρῶντες δυσχεραίνομεν, ἀνδριάντας δὲ καὶ γραφὰς φθισικῶν ἡδέως θεώμεθα τῷ τὴν διάνοιαν ὑπὸ τῶν μιμημάτων ἄγεσθαι κατὰ τὸ οἰκεῖον.[35]
>
> We feel acute pain at the sight of the sick or the dying; but a painting of Philoctetes or a statue of Jocasta gives us pleasure and elicits our admiration. They say that the artist added silver to Jocasta's face in order to give his bronze statue the appearance of a person on the verge of death. "This, my Epicurean friends," I said, "is really good evidence in favour of the Cyrenaics, who contend in their dispute with you that it is not in our sight or our hearing but in our minds that we receive pleasure from sights and sounds. A hen that cackles ceaselessly or a cawing crow is unpleasant and painful to hear, but the imitator of noisy hens and crows delights us. We are shocked to see consumptives, but we contemplate statues and paintings of them with pleasure, because the mind, by its own nature, is attracted to imitations. (tr. Clement)

Unfortunately we do not know much more about this issue. If we can give full credit to Plutarch's testimony, that according to the Cyrenaics it is the *dianoia* that allows us to experience pleasure, then the connection between Callimachus and the philosophical school of his own country would be even closer, and he could share the same doctrine about the intellectual pleasure derived from artistic imitation. But this is just a suggestion.

[35] Plutarch, Συμποσιακά (*Quaestiones convivales*) 5. 1. 2.

Alongside this text from Plutarch I would also like to quote a meaningful passage from Aristotle concerning the same problem of artistic pleasure, which the philosopher had already distinguished from other types of pleasure:

> περὶ γὰρ τὴν διὰ τῆς ὄψεως ἡδονὴν τῶν καλῶν ἄνευ ἐπιθυμίας ἀφροδισίων, ἢ λύπην τῶν αἰσχρῶν, καὶ περὶ τὴν διὰ τῆς ἀκοῆς τῶν εὐαρμόστων ἢ ἀναρμόστων, ἔτι δὲ πρὸς τὰς δι᾽ ὀσφρήσεως, τάς τε ἀπὸ εὐωδίας καὶ τὰς ἀπὸ δυσωδίας, οὐκ ἔστιν ὁ σώφρων. οὐδὲ γὰρ ἀκόλαστος οὐδεὶς λέγεται τῷ πάσχειν ἢ μὴ πάσχειν. εἰ γοῦν τις ἢ καλὸν ἀνδριάντα θεώμενος ἢ ἵππον ἢ ἄνθρωπον, ἢ ἀκροώμενος ᾄδοντος, μὴ βούλοιτο μήτε ἐσθίειν μήτε πίνειν μήτε ἀφροδισιάζειν, ἀλλὰ τὰ μὲν καλὰ θεωρεῖν τῶν δ᾽ ᾀδόντων ἀκούειν, οὐκ ἂν δόξειεν ἀκόλαστος εἶναι, ὥσπερ οὐδ᾽ οἱ κηλούμενοι παρὰ ταῖς Σειρῆσιν. ἀλλὰ περὶ τὰ δύο τῶν αἰσθητῶν ταῦτα, περὶ ἅπερ καὶ τἆλλα θηρία μόνον τυγχάνει αἰσθητικῶς ἔχοντα, καὶ χαίροντα καὶ λυπούμενα, περὶ τὰ γευστὰ καὶ ἁπτά. περὶ δὲ τὰ τῶν ἄλλων αἰσθητῶν ἡδέα σχεδὸν ὁμοίως ἅπαντα φαίνεται ἀναισθήτως διακείμενα, [1231a] οἷον περὶ εὐαρμοστίαν ἢ κάλλος. οὐθὲν γάρ, ὅ τι καὶ ἄξιον λόγου, φαίνεται πάσχοντα αὐτῇ τῇ θεωρίᾳ τῶν καλῶν ἢ τῇ ἀκροάσει τῶν εὐαρμόστων, εἰ μή τί που συμβέβηκε τερατῶδες: ἀλλ᾽ οὐδὲ πρὸς τὰ εὐώδη ἢ δυσώδη: καίτοι τάς γε αἰσθήσεις ὀξυτέρας ἔχουσι πάσας. ἀλλὰ καὶ τῶν ὀσμῶν ταύταις χαίρουσιν ὅσαι κατὰ συμβεβηκὸς εὐφραίνουσιν, ἀλλὰ μὴ καθ᾽ αὑτάς. λέγω δὲ μὴ καθ᾽ αὑτάς, αἷς ἢ ἐλπίζοντες χαίρομεν ἢ μεμνημένοι, οἷον ὄψων καὶ ποτῶν (δι᾽ ἑτέραν γὰρ ἡδονὴν ταύταις χαίρομεν, τὴν τοῦ φαγεῖν ἢ πιεῖν), καθ᾽ αὑτὰς δὲ οἷον αἱ τῶν ἀνθῶν εἰσίν. διὸ ἐμμελῶς ἔφη Στρατόνικος τὰς μὲν καλὸν ὄζειν τὰς δὲ ἡδύ.[36]
>
> Temperance is not related to pleasure from the sight of beautiful things, unaccompanid by sexual appetite, nor to pain from the sight of ugly things, not to pleasure from listening to harmonious sounds or the pain of cacophony, or from smelling good and bad

[36] Aristoteles, *Ethica Eudemia* III 2, 1230b25–31a12.

> odours. No one is called undisciplined for having or failing to have those experiences. At any rate, no one would be thought undisciplined for contemplating a beautiful statue or beautiful horse or human, or listening to someone singing, with no desire to eat or drink or have sex, but simply in wanting to contemplate those beautiful things and listen to people singing – anymore than those who were spellbound by the Sirens. Temperance, rather, is concerned with the only two kinds of perceptible object that the other animals too happen to be sensitive to and take pleasure in, namely those of taste and touch. Towards the pleasures of other perceptible objects all beasts appear disposed pretty much equally insensitively, for example, regarding harmonious sound or visual beauty. It is evident that they experience nothing of any note through the simple act of looking at beautiful things or hearing harmonious sounds, except perhaps in a few prodigious cases. Nor are they sensitive with regard to good or bad odours, though certainly animal senses are keener than ours. But even with odours the ones they enjoy are those that please them not for their intrinsic qualities but for their incidental associations. By non-intrinsic I mean odours that we enjoy in anticipation or remembrance of things like food and drink, while the pleasure we experience when we enjoy food and drink is a different one, namely that of eating and drinking. By intrinsic I mean odours such as those of flowers. That is what's behind Stratonicus's neat remark that some things smell beautiful and others smell delicious. (tr. Inwood and Woolf, mod. by Destreé)

In reporting the problem of the different types of pleasures and of the specificity of the aesthetic and intellectual pleasure, Aristotle seems to pave the way for the discussions that animated Hellenistic philosophy.[37] In a different context, Cicero reports the dispute between the Hellenistic schools about the superiority of intellectual pleasures, declaring though, follow-

[37] For a discussion of the passage, see P. Destreé, 'Pleasure,' in Id. and P. Murray, *Blackwell Companion to Ancient Aesthetics*, cit., pp. 473-474.

ing the Epicurean doctrine, that they come from the bodily ones:

> Animi autem voluptates et dolores nasci fatemur e corporis voluptatibus et doloribus—itaque concedo, quod modo dicebas, cadere causa, si qui e nostris aliter existimant, quos quidem video esse multos, sed imperitos—, quamquam autem et laetitiam nobis voluptas animi et molestiam dolor afferat, eorum tamen utrumque et ortum esse e corpore et ad corpus referri, nec ob eam causam non multo maiores esse et voluptates et dolores animi quam corporis. nam corpore nihil nisi praesens et quod adest sentire possumus, animo autem et praeterita et futura. ut enim aeque doleamus animo, cum corpore dolemus, fieri tamen permagna accessio potest, si aliquod aeternum et infinitum impendere malum nobis opinemur. quod idem licet transferre in voluptatem, ut ea maior sit, si nihil tale metuamus. Iam illud quidem perspicuum est, maximam animi aut voluptatem aut molestiam plus aut ad beatam aut ad miseram vitam afferre momenti quam eorum utrumvis, si aeque diu sit in corpore.[38]
>
> Again, we aver that mental pleasures and pains arise out of bodily ones (and therefore I allow your contention that any Epicureans who think otherwise put themselves out of court; and I am aware that many do, though not those who can speak with authority); but although men do experience mental pleasure that is agreeable and mental pain that is annoying, yet both of these we assert arise out of and are based upon bodily sensations. Yet we maintain that this does not preclude mental pleasures and pains from being much more intense than those of the body; since the body can feel only what is present to it at the moment, whereas the mind is also cognizant of the past and of the future. For, granting that pain of body is equally painful, yet our sensation of pain can be enormously increased by the belief that some evil of unlimited magnitude and duration threatens to befall us

---

[38] Cicero, *De finibus* I 55-56.

> hereafter. And the same consideration may be transferred to pleasure: a pleasure is greater if not accompanied by any appreciation of evil. This therefore clearly appears, that intense mental pleasure or distress contributes more to our happiness or misery than a bodily pleasure or pain of equal duration. (tr. Rackham)

Cicero here takes the view that the intellectual pleasure and pain are more intense, of course in a more general context than the concept expressed by Callimachus, but that in any way it expresses the same interest.

Poetry and thambos

We can affirm that it is likely that Callimachus, in proclaiming the preeminence of hearing on the other senses, and in outlining the unlimited duration of the intellectual pleasures, engages in a controversy that concerned the thought of Cyrenaics and the Epicureans and in general the Hellenistic schools. It is indeed more than plausible that Callimachus knew of these debates and that is why, in the specific context of the fragment 43, we might see a reference, controversial or not, to the doctrine of Cyrenaics. We know that a lot has been lost that could clarify our knowledge of the literary disputes and of the importance of the philosophical reflection on poetry and the role of poets. From the fragments of the writings of literary criticism of Philodemus of Gadara[39] we are informed that an extensive literature on the subject existed, but the desperate condition of the papyri prevents us from clearly reconstructing the points on which the disputes were centred. What is clear is that Callimachus, both as a poet and as a theorist, was a key figure in this long and unfortunately obscure series of writings, from

[39] Cf. R. Janko (ed.), *Philodemus. On Poems* I, Oxford 2003, pp. 120-189.

the classical up to the imperial age, which saw the contributions of names like Crates, with the dispute on the superiority of sound on sense in poetry, and Heraclides of Pontus, along with other authors otherwise unknown such as Pausimachus of Miletus, which seems to defend the same mix of genres that Callimachus adopted in his poetry.

Callimachus undoubtedly remains within the boundaries of poetic production and can not be considered in any way a philosopher. That said, it is nevertheless clear that he had a strong interest in philosophical writings, especially those of Plato, and in general his philological attitude corresponds at least to certain trends of the time, undoubtedly influenced by the Peripatetic teachings, which underlayed the foundation of the *Mouseion* in Alexandria. Callimachus is therefore not a philosopher. However, as a poet and philologist he was a competent reader of those texts, for example Platonic, that we now tend to read only as philosophical, and that for him were rather sources for arguments of literary criticism. From this point of view, in those verses from his main poem transmitted from antiquity, Callimachus appears to be a participant and often indeed the protagonist of the cultural debates of his era.

I would like to end quoting another couplet from the fragment 43:

> ὣ[ς] ἡ μὲν λίπε μῦθον, ἐγὼ δ' ἐπὶ καὶ [τὸ πυ]θέσθαι
> ἤ]θελον—ἦ γάρ μοι θάμβος ὑπετρέφ[ετ]ο—, (85)[40]

> Thus she ended her story, but I wanted to know this as well
> – for, truly, my amazement was fed while she spoke –
> (tr. Harder)

[40] Callimachus, *Aitia* fr. 43.84-5.

Once the Muse finished her narration of remote myths concerning the founding of the Sicilian cities, Callimachus expressed his *thambos* at what she had told him, but in fact – in a play of mirrors which reflects Callimachus' poetic approach – it is the reader who is invited to experience *thambos* (that is the feeling of amazement and awe in the presence of the prodigious feats of gods and heroes in the epic tradition) because of Callimachus' exceptional erudition and poetic skill, and also – in our case – his irreverent but competent attitude towards philosophy. And, like the poet himself, we wish we could know more.

MANUM DE TABULA SCIRE TOLLERE
DILIGENTIA AND *NON-FINITO* IN RENAISSANCE

The issue of when precisely a work of art should be considered complete was a topic of discussion in antiquity and it arose again, in relation to the creative process, in the Renaissance, when two opposing positions were to be found, one advocating extreme diligence in applying the finishing touches, on the one hand, and one preferring a more unresolved and spontaneous approach, on the other. What will be investigated here is the possibility of finding links between the attitude of some artists and writers to different degrees of refinement or revision of their work and their engagement with Neoplatonic ideas and culture.

The choice of the appropriate point at which to stop when finishing a work of art is an inherent aspect of artistic practice, which not only concerns figurative arts but also extends to literary activity. It does not seem to apply to architecture, since it essentially concerns the creative process and the execution by a single person, and therefore does not include other, more collaborative forms of art and craftsmanship. The issue is of great interest from the point of view of aesthetics, as it investigates problems and reveals attitudes through different ages and in response to different cultural conditions. Another important aspect to be considered is the need of the adoption of an interdisciplinary approach in order to interpret an artistic phenomenon which, while recognized and investigated as a fact in the framework of art history scholarship, has not been attributed to a specific cultural sphere. The comparison of different disciplines such as art history, literature, philosophy and aesthetics allows a more comprehensive vision of the problem not only during the Renaissance but also in its roots in classical and late ancient culture.

Although the idea that the individual artist has a choice in deciding the level of finish in their work seems to be conceivable only within the mind set of the modern era, the difficulty of identifying the point at which an artwork should be considered finished was discussed already during antiquity. The need to conceal the artistic effect through a certain carelessness is crucial to many modern and contemporary artforms but in fact it has its roots in the aesthetic reflection of antiquity.[1] This is notoriously stated by Pliny the Elder, when he tells of a dispute in which the painter Apelles criticises his rival Protogenes for being excessively accurate in finishing his paintings, to the detriment of the final effect:

> dixit enim omnia sibi cum illo paria esse aut illi meliora, sed uno se praestare, quod manum de tabula sciret tollere, memorabili praecepto nocere saepe nimiam diligentiam.[2]
>
> for he said that in all respects his achievements and those of Protogenes were on a level, or those of Protogenes were superior, but that in one respect he stood higher, that he knew when to take his hand away from a picture — a noteworthy warning of the frequently evil effects of excessive diligence.

This anecdote, regardless of its historical veracity, confirms that the question of when a work of art was considered to be finished constituted one of the elements in the aesthetic debates of classical Greece and was reiterated in Rome. Else-

[1] See P. D'Angelo, *Sprezzatura: Concealing the Effort of Art from Aristotle to Duchamp*, New York 2018.
[2] Pliny, *Nat. Hist.* 35, 80.

where too Pliny, translating into Latin some specific terms of Greek rhetoric criticism such as *charis* and *akribeia* or *ponos*, mentions how excessive overworking and effort[3] can affect the grace and beauty of an artwork, as in the case of Callimachus, the 5th century sculptor:

> Callimachus, semper calumniator sui nec finem habentis diligentiae, ob id *catatexitechnus* appellatus, memorabili exemplo adhibendi et curae modum. huius sunt saltantes Lacaenae, emendatum opus, sed in quo gratiam omnem diligentia abstulerit.[4]

> Callimachus, who was unfairly critical of his own work, was an artist of neverending assiduity and for this reason he is called *catatexitechnus* (*the one who spoils his art by overelaboration*) and is a notable warning of the duty of observing moderation even in the artistic effort. To him belongs the Laconian Women Dancing, a very finished work but one in which assiduity has destroyed all charm.

In the Hellenistic and Imperial age, we can find two opposite stances in this respect, that of poets like Callimachus of Cyrene, who was an advocate of extreme refinement and preciousness in poetry,[5] and, on the other hand, Pseudo-Longinus' observations (*De subl.* 33-36) indicating an awareness of the aesthetic effect produced through neglect of formal perfection in writing.

It is in oratory that the issue of when to stop before ruining the aesthetic impact is addressed with a rationally stated expres-

---

[3] Cf. E.E. Perry, 'Notes on *Diligentia* as a Term of Roman Art Criticism,' in *Classical Philology*, 95, 4 (2000), pp. 445-458.

[4] Pliny, *Nat. Hist.* 34, 92.

[5] Cf. e.g. Callimachus, *Hymn. ad Apoll.* 105-113; *Aitia* fr. 1 Pf. See the first essay in this book.

sion. Cicero, discussing the virtues of the orator, stresses that a good public speech needs to avoid any excessive formal care in order to reach its point and sound as natural as possible, through a specific *negligentia diligens*,[6] a studied casualness which makes a speech effective. Note, however, how the oxymoron itself betrays the writer's propensity for rhetoric effects.

All these examples deal with properly aesthetic judgements on the beauty and appropriateness of a work of art. However, I would like to draw attention to a singular justification for the absence of revision or reworking of a text or of an artwork. In a different context (but one which is fundamental to understanding some of the positions held in the Renaissance) it is of great interest to observe Plotinus' attitude to philosophical writing. According to the testimony of his disciple and biographer Porphyry (*Vita Plot.*, 8, 1-4): Γράψας γὰρ ἐκεῖνος δὶς τὸ γραφὲν μεταλαβεῖν οὐδέποτ' ἂν ἠνέσχετο, ἀλλ' οὐδὲ ἅπαξ γοῦν ἀναγνῶναι καὶ διελθεῖν.[7] 'After writing [Plotinus] could not bear to go back to his work even for one re-reading'. Various interpretations have been offered of Porphyry's statement but it seems that, apart from other reasons including physical problems related to the loss of sight,[8] the author confided in the inspiration of the moment, which has a strength and an efficacy that extend not only to the philosophical content but also to the form that conveys it, giving an aesthetic value to

---

[6] Cicero, *Orator* 78.

[7] Cf. H.D. Saffrey, 'Pourquoi Porphyre a-t-il édité Plotin? Réponse provisoire,' in Porphyre, *La Vie de Plotin. II: Études d'introduction, texte grec et traduction française, commentaire, notes complémentaires, bibliographie*, ed. L. Brisson et al., Paris 1992, pp. 31-64.

[8] Cf. D. O'Brien, 'Comment écrivait Plotin ? Étude sur la *Vie de Plotin* 8. 1-4,' dans Porphyre, *La Vie de Plotin I*, ed. by L. Brisson et al., Paris 1982, pp. 350-351.

his writings.[9] This is connected to the Platonic tradition, in particular to the exegesis of the *Phaedrus*, and characterizes Plotinian and, more generally, Neoplatonic spirituality, especially as recovered and revived by Marsilio Ficino.[10]

Remaining faithful to the inspiration of the moment is, at its core, a spiritual attitude which seems to provide an element of analogy between Plotinus' intellectual procedure and certain attitudes of Renaissance artists belonging to a cultural sphere which has more or less direct links to the Platonic tradition[11] and specifically to Plotinus. When the dilemma of establishing the point of completion re-emerged during the Renaissance, it assumed new and complex meanings depending on the personality of individual artists or men of letters, as well as the cultural circumstances in which they lived.[12]

First of all, we should consider Vasari's comment about Fra' Angelico:

---

[9] For Plotinus' views on art and beauty, cf. O. Kuisma, *Art or Experience: a study on Plotinus' Aesthetics*, Helsinki 2003. See also V.O. Lobsien and C. Olk (edd.), *Neuplatonismus und Äesthetik. Zur Transformationsgeschichte des Schönen*, Berlin-New York 2007.

[10] On the influence of Ficino's neoplatonism on Renaissance art and culture, cf. Allen, M.J.B. Allen, *Synoptic Art: Marsilio Ficino on the History of Platonic Interpretation, Firenze* 1998; also Id. and V. Rees, with M. Davies, *Marsilio Ficino: his Theology, his Philosophy, his Legacy*, Leiden-Boston 2002.

[11] A survey on the reception of Platonism during Renaissance and its limits in G. Kraye, 'The Transformation of Platonic Love in the Italian Renaissance,' in A. Baldwin and S. Hutton (edd.), *Platonism and the English Imagination*, Cambridge 1994, pp. 76-85.

[12] For the Renaissance reflection on the role of the inspired artists, see P.A. Emison, *Creating the "Divine" Artist: From Dante to Michelangelo*, Leiden 2004. See also E. Panofsky, *Idea. A Concept in Art Theory*, Columbia, SC. 1968.

> Aveva per costume non ritoccare, né racconciar mai alcuna sua dipintura, ma lasciarle sempre in quel modo che erano venute la prima volta, per creder (secondo ch'egli diceva) che così fusse la volontà di Dio.[13]
>
> It was his habit never to retouch or alter any of his paintings, but to leave them as they came the first time, believing, as he said, that such was the will of God.

The similarity between Angelico's approach and Plotinus' reluctance to revise his writings is certainly worthy of attention. We cannot infer direct connections between Angelico and Plotinus' thought, since Angelico could not read Plotinus[14] (nor, for that matter, could Vasari) and his knowledge of theology must be most likely confined to the Dominican tradition, however it must be noted that the Greek manuscript which Ficino later used for his translation of the *Enneads* was held in the library of the convent of San Marco where Angelico lived and worked for many years. Nonetheless, it can be argued that a general attitude of regarding the result of one's own work as somehow derived from a divine principle, and thus to be accepted in its original outcome, without changing or forcing its form, is rooted in the late ancient concept of divine inspiration, based on Neoplatonic notions that were transmitted to the Western Middle Ages mainly by Augustine.[15]

---

[13] Cfr. G. Vasari, *Vita di fra' Giovanni da Fiesole dell'Ordine de' Frati Predicatori, Pittore*, in *Le vite de' più eccellenti pittori, scultori, e architettori*, [Firenze 1567] Roma 1991, p. 385.

[14] On Angelico's cultural references, see L. Castelfranchi Vegas, *L'Angelico e l'Umanesimo*, Milano 1989.

[15] On the influence of Neoplatonism on Christianity, see M. Di Pasquale Barbanti and C. Martello (edd.), *Neoplatonismo pagano vs. Neoplatonismo cristiano. Identità e intersezioni*, atti del Seminario Internazionale di Catania, 25-26 Settembre 2004, Catania 2006. See also D. Hadley and S.

As daring as this comparison might seem – although it has been pointed out that already in the mid-fifteenth century the attention of the humanists in Florence was turning to Platonism in general, and Angelico himself might have had connections with this phenomenon[16] - it might shed some light also on the ultimately mystical motivations in Plotinus for not revising his writings.

It must be mentioned that Vasari was well aware of Pliny's remarks and he considers certain aspects of *facilità* (dexterity and carelessness) as signs of good art, in the same manner as Castiglione favoured *sprezzatura* in the manners of his ideal gentleman.[17] This appreciation, however, is not necessarily connected to the idea of a spiritual origin of the artistic activity itself, unlike in Angelico and, for philosophy, in Plotinus.

Another connection – this time explicit – between Plotinus' attitude to writing and a Renaissance writer, in the wish to abstain from reviewing what has been written, can be found in the case of Torquato Tasso. He read and admired the Neoplatonic philosopher[18] and drew attention to Porphyry's account of Plotinus' method of writing in a letter to Scipione Gonzaga, stating that he found in Plotinus a precedent for his own negli-

---

Hutton, (edd.), *Platonism at the Origins of Modernity. Studies on Platonism and Early Modern Philosophy*, Dordrecht 2008.

[16] Cfr. J.T. Spike, *Angelico*, Milano 1996, pp. 60-69.

[17] Cf. C.M. Serrano, 'Facilità y non finito en las vidas de Vasari,' in *EGA: revista de expresión gráfica arquitectónica* 9 (2004), pp. 58-67. Cf. also P. Burke, *The Fortunes of the Courtier: The European Reception of Castiglione's* Cortegiano, Cambridge 2007^3.

[18] On Plotinus' influence in the XVI century, see M. Muccillo, 'Plotino nel tardo Rinascimento,' in Ead., *Platonismo, ermetismo e «prisca theologia». Ricerche di storiografia filosofica rinascimentale*, Firenze 1996, pp. 195-289.

gence in correcting his writings:[19]

> Prego Vostra Signoria a legger questi tre ultimi (canti) come cosa imperfettissima. La prego anco a non mostrarli ad alcuno, se ben può leggerli a chi vuole; perchè sarebbe gran vergogna la mia, che fossero visti così male scritti, con tante cancellature e con tanti errori di penna quanti vi debbono essere; e ho gran dubbio che Vostra Signoria stessa non saprà leggerli. Di lei non mi vergogno tanto, sapendo ch'ella, che mi stima sovra il mio merito, attribuisce alcuna sorte d'errori più tosto a fretta o a negligenza ch'ad ignoranza; ma gli altri, giudicandomi dalle mie scritture, mi potrebbono riputare un grande ignorante. Pur mi consola l'aver letto che Plotino, del quale nissun mai più dotto o eloquente uscì dalle scole platoniche, scriveva scorrettissimamente e non sapea alcuna regola d'ortografia.[20]

> I pray Your Lordship to read these last three (*canti*) as a most imperfect thing. I also beg you not to show them to anyone, although you can read them to whomever you want; as I should be greatly ashamed, that they were seen so badly written, with so many erasures and with so many mistakes; and I greatly wonder if Your Lordship will be able to read them. I am not ashamed of you so much, knowing that you, who esteem me above my merit, attribute any kind of errors rather to haste or negligence than to ignorance; but the other readers, judging me from my writings, could consider me a great ignorant. Although I was consoled by having read that Plotinus (and no one ever more learned or eloquent than him came from the Platonic schools) wrote improperly and knew no spelling rule.

It is interesting that in Tasso such attitude can be described

[19] See E. Ardissino, *Tasso, Plotino, Ficino. In margine a un postillato*, Roma 2003, pp. 16-17.
[20] Torquato Tasso, *Lettere*, ed. by C. Guasti, Firenze 1883-5, I, p. 115.

almost as consciously aesthetic, and his preference for stylistic negligence is further reasserted in the same letter when the poet compares his adoption of *parlar disgiunto* to the method of Virgil in the *Eneid*.

A connection with the Neoplatonic concept of divine inspiration and poetic *furor* is apparent in Michelangelo. His problematic *non-finito*, though at times linked to well-documented external events, also clearly reflect a search for artistic expression.[21] On the one hand, he was never satisfied with his achievements and tried to improve his works without ever arriving at a final result (this is the case with all his late versions of the *Pietà*); on the other hand, this attitude led to the achievement, in his mature works, of a spiritually complete expression, due precisely to the lack of a thorough finish. Michelangelo's position may seem extreme because his avoidance of finishing touches resulted at times in renouncing the definition of the form itself. Nevertheless, it is linked, as an issue related to artistic practice, to the question already raised in antiquity by Apelles; and Michelangelo's position on this matter appears close to that of Plotinus and Fra' Angelico.[22]

The spiritual attitude in leaving the artwork in its first, unadultered expression cannot be identified, however, with the *sprezzatura* of Titian's late works, because in this case it is a deliberate stylistic choice which is not directly intended as the manifestation of a divine inspiration. There are also many examples of artists at the other end of the scale: Lorenzo di

---

[21] Among the vast literature on Michelangelo's approach to art, see R.J. Clements, *Michelangelo's Theory of Art*, New York 1961; D. Summers, *Michelangelo and the Language of Arts*, Princeton 1981.

[22] See my *Aesthetic Themes in Pagan and Christian Neoplatonism*, London 2015, pp. 52-55.

Credi, for instance, whose excessively clean method of painting Vasari deplored; and Pontormo, who worked in the Capponi chapel with many variations and verifications.

The two opposing attitudes towards smoothness and roughness in Renaissance artistic practice cannot easily be connected to a particular view of the world and to the adherence to a specific system of thought. However, it can be helpful to detect the trend in some artists and writers to incline towards one of these two positions. In some significative cases the artist or writer has deliberately chosen to limit the finishing process, and this intention is sometimes related to specific spiritual aspirations and – even if loosely – to their proximity to Neoplatonic culture and spirituality. Angelico, Michelangelo, Tasso, in their desire not to interfere with the source of their inspiration, can be examples of the spiritual roots of the dilemma of whether to strive for formal elegance or, instead, for expressive *negligentia*.

Plotinus' reflection on personal freedom reaches its apex in the treatise VI 8 (39) where, after commenting on a passage from Aristotle's *Ethica Nicomachea* III 1- 5 and having tried to distinguish what can determine freedom in human actions, he investigates the nature of the freedom and will of the One.[1] Bearing in mind the centrality of such reflection within Plotinus' system with regard to his conception of the autonomy of human action and the prerogatives of the individual soul, it could be useful to focus on a passage, certainly secondary but still worthy of interest, in his second treatise on providence. Here, though without explicitly referring to the doctrine of τὰ ἐφ' ἡμῖν (an Aristotelian expression which, according to Francesco Romano,[2] can be understood as *free will*, while others prefer to translate in a less determined way as *what depends on us*),[3] Plotinus seems to offer an example which is clear as well as penetrating from a psychological point of view. In fact, he mentions the difference in attitude of two individuals with respect to the same solicitation, to show how autonomy of choice is present in individuals within the rational order given

[1] For a commentary on the treatise and its sources, particularly Aristotle and Alexander of Aphrodisias, see G. Leroux (ed.), *Plotin. Traité sur la liberté et la volonté de l'Un*, Paris 1990.

[2] Cf. F. Romano, 'Azione morale e libero arbitrio in Plotino. "La virtù non ha padrone" [ἀρετὴ ἀδέσποτον] (Plat., *Rep*. X, 617e 3),' in M. Vegetti e M. Abbate (edd.), *La* Repubblica *di Platone nella tradizione antica*, Napoli 1999, p. 153.

[3] See E. Eliasson, *The Notion of* That Which Depends on Us *in Plotinus and Its Background*, Leiden-Boston 2008, which is devoted to interpretation of Plotinus' doctrine of ἐφ' ἡμῖν. In particolar at pp. 26-43 Eliasson reviews the different possible translations of the Greek expression, and their subsequent philosophical interpretations.

by the providence in the universe. The fact that such solicitation is connected to beauty makes Plotinus' reflection particularly relevant in the context of aesthetic research.

Homeric heroes and free will

The passage I refer to can be found in *Enn.* III 3 (48) 5, 41-43, where Plotinus discusses the different reactions of Paris and Idomeneus to Helen's beauty:

> Οὐ γὰρ τὸ αὐτὸ ποιεῖ πᾶν προσελθὸν ραντί, ἀλλὰ τὸ αὐτὸ πρὸς ἄλλο καὶ ἄλλο πρὸς ἄλλο· οἷον καὶ τὸ τῆς Ἑλένης κάλλος πρὸς μὲν τὸν Πάριν ἄλλο εἰργάζετο, Ἰδομενεὺς δὲ ἔπαθεν οὐ τὸ αὐτό·

> The one circumstance does not produce the same result wherever it acts; the normal operation will be modified from case to case: Helen's beauty told very differently on Paris and on Idomeneus. (tr. MacKenna-Page)[4]

Plotinus introduces this *exemplum*[5] within a context in which he questions the limits of man's freedom with respect to the providential plan. Here this problem, which in the previous treatise seemed to have been resolved through the metaphor of theatre,[6] is again discussed from a different point of view, and Plotinus tries to find a solution to new aporias. In the passage just cited, in particular, he distinguishes between the providen-

---

[4] I use the same translation, sometimes adapted, for the other passages from the *Enneads*.

[5] Plotinus, in Platonic fashion, often uses myths in order express philosophical meanings: cf. T.A. Szlezák, *Platone e Aristotele nella dottrina del* Nous *di Plotino*, Milano 1997, p. 40-41.

[6] Cf. *Enn.* III 2, 15-17. See my *Plotino. La provvidenza*, Enn. *III 2 e III 3*, Roma 2009, pp. 55-68.

tial element and that which depends on the individual, as entrusted to his moral autonomy. The story of the Trojan war had already been the subject of reflection by the Medioplatonic Alcinous,[7] who investigated about individual responsibility and how events are to be considered fatal as a consequence of free actions, as indeed the Trojan war as a result of Paris' abduction of Helen.

Before considering the solution that Plotinus presents to the problem in general, we can try to understand what he says in the passage, which is not immediately evident to the modern reader. Here, two Homeric characters are compared in their reactions[8] (I say reactions, as talking about feelings in the field of the archaic epic is probably incorrect) in front of the same beautiful woman. Since, of the three, both Helen and Paris are widely known, our attention can focus on Idomeneus, who, although illustrious, does not enjoy the fame – fatal or not – of the adulterous couple.

Without dwelling on the reasons for Paris' action for now, and before getting to know better the figure of Idomeneus, there is one element to be observed in Plotinus' affirmation: that is, the protagonists of the action are the two men. Helen's responsibility is not highlighted, as it is her beauty, considered as an objective and natural element, which arouses the different effects. In view of the traditional dispute over Helen's guilt, the

---

[7] Cf. Alcinous, *Didaskalikos* 26, 179, 13-15; see G. Boys-Stones, 'Middle Platonists on Fate and Human Autonomy,' in R.W. Sharples-R. Sorabji (edd.), *Greek and Roman Philosophy from 100 BC to 200 AD*, London, pp. 431-447.

[8] On erotic passion in Plotinus, cf. my *Aesthetic Themes in Pagan and Christian Neoplatonism: from Plotinus to Gregory of Nyssa*, London 2015, pp. 77-84.

fact that Plotinus does not seem to assign her a moral role may appear surprising at first sight.[9] Helen, who is already given some responsibility in the Homeric poems,[10] is often given full blame in following Paris, such as in Aeschyl's insult which defines her as νυμφόκλαυτος Ἐρινύς,[11] "Fury that makes wives cry." However, as it is well known, she is also defended, with different methods and motivations, to cite only the best known examples, by Stesichorus[12] and Euripides[13] with the curious legend that what was in Troy was only her *eidolon*, and by Gorgias[14] in an unconventional (and Sophistic by definition) manner, while Sappho's position[15] is isolated, as she gives Helen full moral responsibility and for this very reason presents her as a model, not considering necessary to justify or defend the actions of her heroine, but rather exalting her because she has chosen and followed the object of her love, even though she already possessed the best that could be had from a common perspective. If all the examples cited above come from the archaic and classical age, that of Lucian,[16] who is still to be counted among the detractors of Helen but who implicitly assigns her a free will, leads us to a temporal and cultural context closer to that of Plotinus.

---

[9] Helen is also mentioned in *Enn.* V 8 (31) 2, 9, *On the intelligible beauty*, and there too for her beauty but not for her personal responsibility.

[10] Cf. Γ 171-176.

[11] Aeschylus, *Ag.* 749.

[12] Cf. Stesichorus, fr. 15 Page. About the *Palinode*, cf. Plato, *Phaedr.* 243a. Stesichorus, fr. 46 Page, which is unfavourable to Helen, must be earlier.

[13] This is the subject of *Helen*.

[14] Cf. G. Basta Donzelli, 'La colpa di Elena. Gorgia ed Euripide a confronto,' in L. Montoneri-F. Romano, *Gorgia e la Sofistica*, Atti del Convegno Internazionale di Lentini-Catania, 12-15 dicembre 1983, Catania 1985, pp. 389-409, repr. in Ead., *Studi sul teatro antico*, Amsterdam 2008, pp. 137-150.

[15] Cf. Sappho, fr. 16 Voigt. Cf. Plato, *Lys.* 211d-e.

[16] Cf. Lucian, *Ver. hist.* II 15.

Therefore, since in the literary tradition the motif of Helen's responsibility or innocence was widespread[17] – it is also present in Plato, for example –, a malevolent reading of Plotinus' text might lead to the conclusion that in the absence of notations on the active role of the woman one could see very little propensity on the part of the philosopher to attribute moral autonomy to the female sex in general. But such suspicion, considering Plotinus' concept of the individual soul, is obviously to discard. In reality, in this specific passage Plotinus' point of view focuses specifically on the behavior of the two men because it is functional to the definition of the attitudes of two different free wills. Helen, therefore, is simply seen in her function as stimulus, to which different reactions are given: if Plotinus had to consider her role too, the explanation of the relationship between universal providence and individual responsibility would have been complicated, while he would have lost the icasticity of the example with the comparison between two different choices in relation to the same situation. A possible accusation of misogyny at the address of Plotinus seems therefore in this case averted.

Once this annotation – which may seem marginal but perhaps constitutes an indication of the difficulty, both for Plotinus, in this case, and generally for the thinkers of antiquity who have posed the same problem, to identify the relationship between individual autonomy and cosmic design – has been made, we can focus on the figure that constitutes the fulcrum of Plotinus' text, as he is presented, at least in relation to Paris, as a moral model. Idomeneus of Crete[18] is one of the heroes of the *Iliad*, where he is mentioned sixty-nine times with his name or

---

[17] On the tradition about Helen, see R. Blondell, *Helen of Troy: Beauty, Myth, Devastation*, Oxford 2015.

[18] Cf. F. Jacoby, *Idomeneus*, *RE* XVII, coll. 906-909.

with the patronymic, Δευκαλίδης,[19] and is also the protagonist of an *aristeia.*[20] As a source for the Plotinus passage, Γ 230-233 is generally mentioned: the context is that in which Helen, questioned by Priam, indicates who the Greek heroes are that the Trojans see from afar, admiring their majesty and beauty.[21] To describe Idomeneus, Helen's words are:

> Ἰδομενεὺς δ' ἑτέρωθεν ἐνὶ Κρήτεσσι θεὸς ὣς
> ἕστηκ', ἀμφὶ δέ μιν Κρητῶν ἀγοὶ ἠγερέθονται.
> πολλάκι μιν ξείνισσεν ἀρηΐφιλος Μενέλαος
> οἴκῳ ἐν ἡμετέρῳ ὁπότε Κρήτηθεν ἵκοιτο.[22]
>
> And Idemeneus on the other side among the Cretans like a god
> and around him are assembled the leaders of the Cretans
> hospitality often has the battle-loving Menelaus entertained him
> with, in our house, when he came from Crete.

Following this indication, we can better understand what Plotinus affirms, in that Idomeneus was frequently a guest of Menelaus and therefore had the opportunity to admire the beauty of Helen, but was respectful of the marital bonds and did no harm to his munificent guest, unlike Paris later on.

---

[19] A 145; B 405, 645, 650; Γ 230; Δ 252, 253, 256, 257; E 43, 45, 48; Z 436; H 165; Θ 78, 263; K 53, 58, 112; Λ 501, 510; M 117; N 210, 219, 221, 232, 240, 248, 255, 259, 274, 297, 304, 311, 330, 362, 370, 384, 387, 402, 405, 424, 434, 439, 445, 467, 469, 470, 476, 500, 502, 506, 509; O 301; Π 345; P 258, 605, 608, 621, 624; T 311; Ψ 113, 124, 450, 474, 493, 528, 860, 888. Also in the *Odissey*: γ 191; ν 260; ξ 237, 382, τ 181, 190.

[20] Cf. N 361-454.

[21] For a comment on the passage, cf. J.N. Ready, *Character, Narrator, and Simile in the* Iliad, Cambridge 2011, pp. 117-119.

[22] Γ 230-233.

If this is what can be obtained from Homer regarding a comparison between the Cretan and the Trojan, the myths about Idomeneus allow us to better understand the sense of Plotinus' words, since there are two elements, among others, which are not explicit in the Homeric text. The first of these consists in the fact that Idomeneus, a beautiful warrior, had been among Helen's suitors before she married Menelaus, as attested by Hyginus.[23] This circumstance sheds more light, compared to the simple information of his stays in Menelaus' palace, on the value, in Plotinus' eyes, of the hero's behavior: he, in fact, had been attracted, at least once, to Helen, so his continence is not to be attributed to a possible indifference, but to a deliberation of an obviously ethical nature. Therefore, for the interpretation of Plotinus' passage, it is necessary to keep in mind this tradition which, despite the impossibility of identifying a precise source for the philosopher, seems to adapt with particular evidence to our passage.

On the other hand, the second element that can be obtained from a survey of the tradition on Idomeneus outside the Homeric poems is that he seems to assume the connotation of an eminent character from an ethical point of view,[24] more than other heroes, even in the context of a conflict with typically tragic characters. One of the legends about him, in fact, attested by Servius in his commentary to Virgil,[25] tells that, returning from Troy and having found himself in danger because of a storm, he vowed to Poseidon to sacrifice, if he could be able to reach land safely, the first being that would come to

---

[23] Cf. Hyginus, *Fab.* 81, 270.

[24] Cf. Quintus Smyrnaeus, *Posthom.*, V 138, where he is assigned the role of judge, with Nestor and Agamemnon, in the dispute between Odysseus and Ajax.

[25] Cf. Servius, *In Verg. Aen.* III 121; XI 264.

meet him on the mainland. However, once the storm had passed, coming down from the ship he met his son, so he was faced with the terrible choice between two impious actions, either to fail the vow or to kill the being that he himself had generated. Preferring not to offend the divinity in a direct way, he decides painfully to sacrifice his son (even if Servius says that he does not know if this action has actually been executed),[26] thus provoking a pestilence among the Cretans, who consequently forced him into an exile[27] during which he arrived in Italy, as Virgil tells.[28] In this context, it is not as much of importance to analyze the characters of the legend in its etiological aspects,[29] as to detect the presence of an ethical evaluation of the character of Idomeneus, a man sincerely religious, though perhaps drawn to blood, and forced to an atrocious choice, according to a *topos* which can be found in the tragic plots and which, as regards the case of human sacrifice, has its most famous example in Euripides' *Iphigenia in Aulis*. The legend of a promised sacrifice, with tragic outcomes, also finds a parallel in the Old Testament where, in Judges XI, 29-40, an analogous account is narrated, having as its protagonist Jephte, who finds himself forced to sacrifice his daughter not to fail the vow he had made.[30]

---

[26] *Ib.* III 121: *Contigit ut filius eiiis primus occurreret: quem cum, ut alii dicunt, immolasset, ut alii vero, immolare voluisset* [...].

[27] In the other passage from Servius (XI 264), the Cretans condemn his cruel action.

[28] Cf. Virgil, *Aen.* III 140s.: *et Sallentinos obsedit milite campos/ Lyctius Idomeneus*. On the different traditions on his exile, see F. Jacoby, *Idomeneus*, cit.

[29] For the role of the myth of Idomeneus in Virgil, cf. E. Dekel, *Virgil's Homeric Lens*, New York-London 2012, pp. 102-103.

[30] Cf. J.Ch. Exum, *Tragedy and Biblical Narrative,* Cambridge 1992, pp. 45-69.

It should also be mentioned, only by way of curiosity, that there is another myth regarding Idomeneus,[31] one in which he is called to judge the beauty of Medea and Thetis: having Idomeneus decided in favour of the latter, Medea curses him with not being able to say anything true; this is to explain the common belief about the propensity of the Cretans to lie. Here Idomeneus does not seem to possess positive connotations from the ethical point of view, apart from the attribution of the role of judge, but it must be considered that the story is part of a series linked to the proverb Κρῆτες ἀεὶ ψεῦσται and is a testimony of some oddities of the scholarly interests in antiquity.[32] We should also mention that the hero has had the honour, within Western culture, of being the protagonist of one of Mozart's operas, *Idomeneo re di Creta*, composed in 1780 with a libretto by Gian Battista Varesco, in which the story of his vow to Neptune is described, with fantasy variants such as the introduction of a love theme and the intervention of a deus ex machina for a happy ending.

Providence and free will

If I have focused on some aspects of the myths concerning Idomeneus it is for a better understanding, at this point, of the words of Plotinus: Idomeneus and Paris are not simply two illustrious guests of Menelaus, as one might derive considering the one passage from the *Iliad* generally reported in the editions of the text. The two heroes are specular, and then anti-

---

[31] Cf. Photius, *Bibl.* 150a-b.

[32] On Idomeneus' fortune in Western culture, cf. M. Valverde Sánchez, 'El mito de Idomeneo, de la épica antigua a la tragedia moderna,' in *Myrtia* XX (2005), pp. 265-291. Particularly important for the popularity of the figure of Idomeneus was Fénelon's *Télémaque* (1699).

thetical, for a deeper reason, that is the admiration and desire that both had for Helen. It is this element (which, as much as I have verified, has not been identified previously), which constitues the specific motivation for Plotinus to compare the two characters in order to define their diversity, since the virtuous one, once the events have brought another man to marry the woman of whom he too had been a suitor, does not violate either the conjugal pacts or the hospitality offered; the other, Paris (who, as already mentioned, had been presented as an example of negative responsibility in Alcinous), behaved in the opposite way. The beauty of Helen, therefore, produces different effects, but not in the sense that we could grasp at first, that one man is taken by passion and the other is not; on the contrary, more probably and in a more coherent way (both with the traditional legends on Idomeneus and with the context of what Plotinus affirms), we must understand the text in the sense that the beauty of Helen, which from an emotional point of view produces similar effects in the two characters, leads to completely different ethical behaviors.

The reference to these characters leads Plotinus to a reflection that takes on general value:

> καὶ ἀκόλαστος ἀκολάστῳ καλὸς καλῷ συμπεσὼν ἄλλο, ὁ δὲ σώφρων καλὸς ἄλλο πρὸς σώφρονα τοιοῦτον· ἢ πρὸς ἀκόλαστον ἄλλο ὁ αὐτός, ὁ δ΄ ἀκόλαστος πρὸς αὐτὸν ἄλλο.[33]
>
> Bring together two handsome people of loose character and two living honourably and the resulting conduct is very different; a good man meeting a libertine exhibits a distinct phase of his nature and, similarly, the dissolute answer to the society of their betters.

[33] *Enn.* III 3, 5, 43-46.

Here too we can observe the fineness of Plotinus' investigation, which seeks to identify possible variations in the encounter between different subjects. It is necessary to reiterate once again that the problem that Plotinus poses in this passage is of a moral nature and concerns the relationship between providence and the freedom of man. We can try to provide a scheme of Plotinus' reasoning: in the first type of relationship there is an ἀκόλαστος, (an individual, therefore, who has a negative moral qualification), which is also καλὸς, a quality which, being linked to the dispositions of nature, should be referred back, in the thought of Plotinus, to the providential design. Such an individual, if he meets another one with the same characteristics, will produce a certain effect. A person who is beautiful, and therefore has the same physical characteristics of the first character, but is otherwise σώφρων, and is therefore the opposite under the moral profile, will produce a completely different effect on those who are like him or her. In the first two examples, then, one has the same characteristic of nature, in this case beauty, which arouses attraction, and opposite moral connotations; the third and fourth examples cross the first two giving rise to other effects: the chaste who is also beautiful has a certain effect on those who are not chaste and vice versa. In the conciseness of Plotinus' writing not all possibilities are taken into consideration, since one can also think of someone ugly who is also chaste or dissolute, but the reason why Plotinus neglects the other hypothetical relations is that only beauty, according to the present example, excite that attraction on which the different moral responses are articulated and linked to the virtue or vice that has been cultivated by the individual.

Summing up, we can say that Plotinus argues that the same physical characteristic (attributable to the order established in nature by the *logos*, through which providence is administered) produces different effects according to the moral qualities of the individual. As a consequence, the range of actions for human freedom is very wide, since moral qualities depend on the individual. If in the first treatise on providence Plotinus had already tried to explain in what sense every man is responsible for his own actions and moral growth, here he resumes the discussion by observing the various possibilities that can be given in life, to which one responds according to whether one is virtuous or not.

In the intersection between providential element and moral choice, then, the freedom of the latter is always preserved. In the *cosmos*, what happens in relation to free human choices can not be traced directly back to providence, since the individual who makes a choice is the only one responsible. If, however, an action is virtuous, it is found to be in conformity with providence, inasmuch as it follows the universal *logos*. In fact, as Plotinus says:

> Καὶ παρὰ μὲν τοῦ ἀκολάστου τὸ πραχθὲν οὔτε ὑπὸ προνοίας οὔτε κατὰ πρόνοιαν, τὸ δ´ ὑπὸ τοῦ σώφρονος ἔργον οὐχ ὑπὸ προνοίας μέν, ὅτι ὑπ´ αὐτοῦ, κατὰ πρόνοιαν δέ· σύμφωνον γὰρ τῷ λόγῳ, ὥσπερ καὶ ὃ ὑγιεινῶς πράξειεν ἄν τις αὐτὸς πράξας κατὰ λόγον τὸν τοῦ ἰατροῦ. Τοῦτο γὰρ καὶ ὁ ἰατρὸς παρὰ τῆς τέχνης ἐδίδου εἴς τε τὸ ὑγιαῖνον εἴς τε τὸ κάμνον. Ὃ δ´ ἄν τις μὴ ὑγιαῖνον ποιῇ, αὐτός τε ποιεῖ καὶ παρὰ τὴν πρόνοιαν τοῦ ἰατροῦ εἰργάσατο.[34]
>
> The act of the libertine is not done by providence or in accordance with providence; neither is the action of the good done by providence – it is done by the man – but it is done in accordance

---

[34] *Enn.* III 3, 5, 46-54.

> with providence, for it is an act consonant with the *logos*. Thus a patient following his treatment is himself an agent and yet is acting in accordance with the doctor's method inspired by the art concerned with the causes of health and sickness: what one does against the laws of health is one's act, but an act conflicting with the *pronoia* of medicine.

The *logos*, in fact, certainly determines that virtuous actions are those which should performed, while bad actions damage the individual who perpetrates them as well as those around him and the physical *cosmos* itself: we should consider that, in Plotinus' passage, the context is that of Paris' debauchery, which had led to a war harmful to all. To say that a virtuous action is in conformity with the universal *logos*, therefore, equates to demonstrate that human happiness is attainable if, through actions that are the result of free choices, one accords with the plans of the *logos*.

At this point it is necessary to make a very brief reference to the role that Plotinus assigns to such *logos*, according to what emerges from the two treatises dedicated to providence. It is in them, in fact, that Plotinus develops a doctrine of the *logos* that assumes entirely specific traits and which in the past had led scholars to think, in addition to an evident presence of Stoic thought (which is also in the background in the two treatises) also of a possible influence of Philo,[35] which can not be clearly demonstrated but is certainly possible as well as suggestive.

---

[35] Cf. A.H. Armstrong, *The Architecture of the Intelligible Universe in the Philosophy of Plotinus*, Cambridge 1949, p. 107s.; a different position in J. Rist, *Plotinus. The Road to Reality*, Cambridge 1967, p. 84-102.

The function that Plotinus assigns to the *logos* is complex, since it is connected to the soul and its productive function on the one hand, and on the other it is related to the *nous*.[36] Here we can only make a reference to the question of whether the *logos* should be given a hypostatic character, which it seems to assume in the treatises providence. In general, however, this position seems to be rejected by Plotinus, given the fact that he explicitly opposes it in the treatise *Against the Gnostics*, *Enn.* II 9 (33), where he affirms that there is no possibility of another intermediate reality between intellect and soul, because if we were to place further median levels we would deny the capacity itself for the soul to think.[37] Since therefore the *logos* can not be considered a hypostasis, but it does seem to assume semi-hypostatic characters in III 2 and 3, it could be possible that in Plotinus it expresses a mediating function at the level of all realities (since, as emphasized by Couloubaritsis,[38] it has a function related to the One) and, consequently, allows the relationship between the different hypostases and between these and the world.

To affirm that providence is effected by means of the *logos* poses to Plotinus the problem, which the Stoics already faced, of reconciliating human freedom with the belief in a rational design aimed at the universal good. This is, as already said, the the context in which Plotinus proposes the example of Idomeneus and Paris, in order to illustrate the distinct fields of action for providence and for man. Although in the first treatise on

---

[36] On *logos* in the two treatises on providence, see my *Plotino. La provvidenza*, cit., pp. 39-49.

[37] Cf. *Enn.* II 9 (33) 1, 33 e 57-63.

[38] Cf. L. Couloubaritsis, 'Le Logos hénologique chez Plotin,' in M.O. Goulet-Cazé, G. Madec, D. O'Brien (edd.), *ΣΟΦΙΗΣ ΜΑΙΗΤΟΡΕΣ. Chercheurs de Sagesse. Hommage à Jean Pépin*, Paris 1992, pp. 231-243.

providence it seemed that a solution to the problem had been found, at the end of it new questions emerge that need to be answered. To better understand the functions of the *logos*, Plotinus compares it to the author and director of a theatrical play, who inserts in his work different elements, positive and negative, which all together contribute to the success of the representation. The concept expressed in the passage on Idomeneus takes the same issue from a different perspective, accentuating in this case the human freedom which, if well guided and correctly educated (this is how implicitly it can be considered on the basis of the difference between the two characters), leads to agreeing with the *logos*, otherwise it produces free acts which, in an immediate manner, are contrary to the providential design but which, thanks to the dispositions and the activity of the *logos*, indirectly also contribute to the cosmic good, since Plotinus' basic assumption is that in any case there is a providence[39] and this is implemented universally even through events and actions which appear to be contrary to it.[40]

It should still be remembered that Plotinus' reflection on human freedom has its roots in the Platonic and Aristotelian speculation. Certainly it was Aristotle who first tried to distinguish with greater attention the various aspects linked to human will and freedom: suffice it to recall that in the *Nicomachean Ethic* he establishes a vocabulary of moral action.[41] It is probably through the influence of Alexander of Aphrodisias that Plotinus reads Aristotle's reflection on ἐφ' ἡμῖν as already in Alexander a fusion seems to have been

[39] Cf. *Enn.* III 2 (47) 1, 3.
[40] Cf. *e.g. ib.* III 2 (47) 2, 25-31; 5, 8-15; 15, 1-20.
[41] Cf. Aristotle, *Eth. Nic.* III 1, 1110b 18ss.; III 2, 1111b 26-30; III 3, 1112a 21ss. Cf. F. Romano, *Azione morale e libero arbitrio in Plotino*, cit., pp. 151-160.

made (which according to Suzanne Bobzien[42] would not have led to a distinct definition of what freedom is) between the Aristotelian and the Stoic and Medioplatonic positions on the question. It could also be noted that, in an accurate study such as that of Eliasson on the notion of ἐφ' ἡμῖν in Plotinus, the reference to passages such as the one under examination, which does not use the expression entered in the common vocabulary, is not included – though understandibly[43] –in the philosophical survey on personal freedom, even if they deal with the same question.

It is evident that if there is something which depends on us, for which we can act in full freedom, there is also something else on which we have no power. Plotinus' reflection on this differs from that of the Hellenistic philosophers, the Stoics in particular but also the Medio-Platonists,[44] as he believes that all that does not fall under the action of human freedom should not be interpreted as destiny, but as πρόνοια. This concept, beyond the references to Aristotle and Alexander regarding human freedom, appears to be first of all derived from Plato

---

[42] Cf. S. Bobzien, 'The Inadvertent Conception and Late Birth of the Free-Will Problem,' in *Phronesis* XLIII (1998), pp. 133-175.

[43] Cf. E. Eliasson, *The Notion of* That Which Depends on Us *in Plotinus and Its Background*, cit., pp. 18-20.

[44] The concept of conditional fate in Ps. Plutarco, *De fat.* 568C-D, (and also in Alcinous, *Did.* 26; Calcidius, *In Tim.* 142-144) is discussed in R.W. Sharples, 'The Stoic Background to the Middle Platonist Discussion of Fate,' in M. Bonazzi-Ch. Helmig (edd.), *Platonic Stoicism – Stoic Platonism. The Dialogue between Platonism and Stoicism in Antiquity*, Leuven 2008, pp. 169-188. See also J. Opsomer, 'The Middle Platonic doctrine of conditional fate,' in P. d'Hoine and G. Van Riel (edd.), *Fate, Providence and moral responsibility in Ancient, Medieval and Early Modern thought*, Leuven 2014, pp. 137-168.

and the indications of *Resp.* X 617e, concerning the freedom and responsibility of souls in choosing the type of life.

Since here it is not necessary to retrace Plotinus' doctrine on freedom, I will only point out some aspects that Plotinus emphasizes in the dialectic between the autonomy of human action and providence in the two treatises dedicated to the issue. The conception of providence as the rational plane of the universe – which turns everything, including the negative aspects, the physical evils, that is, and the moral ones, towards the good – is deeply consistent with the entire doctrinal construction of Plotinus' thought, and it is for this reason that, notwithstanding the *aporias* which his reflection encounters, the philosopher, in the treatises dedicated to providence, does not give up trying to prove it. If already at the beginning of Enn. III 2, in fact, he rejects as absurd even the only hypothesis that there is not a providence, in the course of the discussion, after having made a rather unusual exaltation of the goodness and beauty of the sensible world, his attention is focused on the problem of reconciling human autonomy with providential action that is sovereign.

The problem posed in the context of the passage about Idomeneus and Paris is, more specifically, that of how to be able to distinguish, on the one hand, the different levels of providence, and on the other the connection of this with human freedom. He introduces a first example, relative to the effects of an action on a being, in this case an animal:

> Καὶ δὴ καὶ οὑτωσὶ πληγέντα οὕτως ἐφθέγξατο τὰ φωνήεντα, τὰ δὲ σιωπῇ πάσχει καὶ κινεῖται τὰ ἀκόλουθα, καὶ ἐκ τῶν φθόγγων ἁπάντων καὶ ἐκ τῶν παθημάτων καὶ ἐνεργημάτων μία τοῦ ζῴου οἷον φωνὴ καὶ ζωὴ καὶ βίος· καὶ γὰρ καὶ τὰ μόρια διάφορα ὄντα

καὶ διάφορον τὴν ἐνέργειαν ἔχοντα· ἄλλο γὰρ ποιοῦσι πόδες, ὀφθαλμοὶ δ᾽ ἄλλο, διάνοια δὲ ἄλλο καὶ νοῦς ἄλλο.[45]

Strike (an animal), and what is designed for utterance gives forth the appropriate volume of sound while other parts take the blow in silence but react in their own especial movement; the total of all the utterance and action and receptivity constitutes what we may call the personal voice, life and history of the living form. The parts, distinct in kind, have distinct functions: the feet have their work and the eyes theirs; the understanding serves to one end, the Intellectual Principle to another.

To any given action, such as a blow, therefore follows a reaction in the animal. This reaction is not a single one, since there are different answers, one from the phonetic organs, other ones from the rest of the living being. The parts not equipped with sound react in silence but they also clearly give a response. The motivation for which Plotinus gives this example is however found in its conclusion, which shows important indications regarding the articulation of the providence: the set of different responses of the organs of the animal gives rise to a reaction that is unitary, in response to a solicitation that is unique. Consequently, as Plotinus says:

Ἓν δὲ ἐκ πάντων καὶ πρόνοια μία· εἱμαρμένη δὲ ἀπὸ τοῦ χείρονος ἀρξαμένη, τὸ δὲ ὑπεράνω πρόνοια μόνον.[46]

But all sums to a unity, a comprehensive Providence. From the inferior grade downwards is *Heimarmene*: the upper is *Pronoia* alone.

[45] *Enn.* III 3, 5, 8-14.
[46] *Ib.* III 3, 5, 14-16.

Therefore providence could be understood as the unitary response that is produced in reaction to certain events, which in some way are adverse to the order established by the *logos*. Plotinus, in fact, also uses another reference to the medical field: just as in living beings there is a *logos*, for which a wounded part heals in a natural way, so it also happens on a universal level.[47] Even this similarity, obviously, has its limits, as there are wounds that can not heal naturally and need external interventions and supports; but what Plotinus means is that there is an action that responds to a rational design and that causes even the negative aspects of the universe to be reconciled to the common good. This, which is a position that can already be traced in the Stoics, assumes a peculiar character in Plotinus, in accordance with his general vision.

Universal harmony through discordant notes

In asserting that providence, at a lower level, is fate, Plotinus makes a reprise of that same concept that in *Enn*. III 1 (3), at the beginning of his written production, he had on the contrary criticized. But in that context it was the deterministic conception which was criticised, while the passage of *Enn*. III 3 can be understood in the sense that there is an apparent necessity that governs the world at the lower level. The fact that the upper level is governed by providence does not pose any difficulty; placing fate at the lower level of the sensible world leads instead to a series of questions, the first of which is to understand if the human soul, in its lower part, is subject to

[47] Cf. *Ib*. III 3, 5, 29-32: οἷον ἐν ἑνὶ σώματι ὑγιείας δοθείσης κατὰ πρόνοιαν τοῦ ζῴου, γενομένης τομῆς καὶ ὅλως τραύματος, πάλιν ἐφεξῆς ὁ λόγος ὁ διοικῶν συνάπτοι καὶ συνάγοι καὶ ἰῷτο καὶ διορθοῖτο τὸ πονῆσαν.

such εἱμαρμένη. It would seem, in this case, that Plotinus, in establishing a specific area for destiny, made a sort of concession to the Stoic position, without articulating this affirmation with the rest of his doctrine.

Just before the passage on Paris and Idomeneus, Plotinus reflects:

> Ὥστε τὰ κακὰ ἑπόμενα εἶναι, ἐξ ἀνάγκης δέ· καὶ γὰρ παρ᾽ ἡμῶν κατ᾽ αἰτίας οὐχ ὑπὸ τῆς προνοίας ἠναγκασμένων, ἀλλ᾽ ἐξ αὐτῶν συναψάντων μὲν τοῖς τῆς προνοίας καὶ ἀπὸ προνοίας ἔργοις, τὸ δὲ ἐφεξῆς συνεῖραι κατὰ βούλησιν ἐκείνης οὐ δυνηθέντων, ἀλλὰ κατὰ τὴν τῶν πραξάντων ἢ κατ᾽ ἄλλο τι τῶν ἐν τῷ παντί, μηδ᾽ αὐτοῦ κατὰ πρόνοιαν πεπραχότος ἢ πεποιηκότος τι ἐν ἡμῖν πάθος.[48]
>
> In sum, evil belongs to the sequence of things, but it comes from necessity. It originates in ourselves; it has its causes no doubt, but we are not, therefore, forced to it by Providence: some of these causes we adapt to the operation of Providence and of its subordinates, but with others we fail to make the connection; the act instead of being ranged under the will of Providence consults the desire of the agent alone or of some other element in the Universe, something which is either itself at variance with Providence or has set up some such state of variance in ourselves.

At this point there is an affirmation which is obviously central for Plotinus' view of man and of virtue: the good, virtuous and consequently happy life is, in a certain sense, the most natural possible, as it follows with docility the rational designs of providence and relates man directly to the higher principles.

---

[48] *Ib.* III 3, 5, 33-40.

However, the problem of how to justify moral evil remains. This seems to be due to the fact that Plotinus' position keeps its reference point in the Socratic-Platonic intellectualism, with the limits and the *aporias* that it entails. We know that in matter and in corporeality Plotinus identifies at the metaphysical level the reasons of evil, but also in that case his position is not without ambiguity, since matter itself can not be considered evil, as it is still derived from the procession the One. It is the inclination towards it which proves to be the cause of evil, and consequently the issue of evil falls exclusively within the moral sphere.[49] In this way, even in the midst of difficulties, a certain coherence seems to emerge in Plotinus' reasoning. The motivations for inclination to matter first on the Soul's part and then in the individual souls are to be found, again, in the solutions that Plato had tried to give. Plotinus' answer seems to be struggling between acceptance – which could be defined as dogmatic – of the Platonic datum and the affirmation of his own monism which is in many ways of a profoundly different nature.

Freedom and necessity therefore remain the two poles within which Plotinus' reflection on ethics is articulated. He does not seem to reach a solution that properly allows a coherent reading of what, in his vision, always remains in a state of irreconcilability. The reasons for this *débâcle* are probably related to what has already been noted about the difficulty of justifying both the goodness of the world as the outcome of the procession and the need to find a cause for the evils that are observed in the soul: perhaps we need to identify in the monistic architecture of Plotinus' thought[50] the reason why he finds no place

[49] Cf. A. Linguiti, 'La materia dei corpi: sullo pseudoilomorfismo plotiniano,' in *Quaestio* 7 (2007), pp. 105-122.
[50] Cf. *ib.*, p. 121-122.

for that which, in reality, is actually experienced. For a Platonist like him, moreover, it remained fundamental to safeguard the freedom of judgment and action of the individual soul, with a view to its destiny after death. This conception, however, seems to contradict Plotinus' view according to which all oppositions are healed in a system that could be defined as symphonic, following the reflection present in another passage of the first treatise on providence, which celebrates the intrinsic necessity and rationality of the diversity of the individual sounds and voices, which represent the various beings:

> ἐκεῖ δὲ ἐξ ἑνὸς λόγου ἡ τῶν διαστατῶν μάχη· ὥστε μᾶλλον ἄν τις τῇ ἁρμονίᾳ τῇ ἐκ μαχομένων εἰκάσειε, καὶ ζητήσει διὰ τί τὰ μαχόμενα ἐν τοῖς λόγοις. Εἰ οὖν καὶ ἐνταῦθα ὀξὺ καὶ βαρὺ ποιοῦσι λόγοι καὶ συνίασιν εἰς ἕν, ὄντες ἁρμονίας λόγοι, εἰς αὐτὴν τὴν ἁρμονίαν, ἄλλον λόγον μείζονα, ὄντες ἐλάττους αὐτοὶ καὶ μέρη, ὁρῶμεν δὲ καὶ ἐν τῷ παντὶ τὰ ἐναντία, οἷον λευκὸν μέλαν, θερμὸν ψυχρόν, καὶ δὴ πτερωτὸν ἄπτερον, ἄπουν ὑπόπουν, λογικὸν ἄλογον, πάντα δὲ ζῴου ἑνὸς τοῦ σύμπαντος μέρη, καὶ τὸ πᾶν ὁμολογεῖ ἑαυτῷ τῶν μερῶν πολλαχοῦ μαχομένων, κατὰ λόγον δὲ τὸ πᾶν, ἀνάγκη καὶ τὸν ἕνα τοῦτον λόγον ἐξ ἐναντίων λόγον εἶναι ἕνα, τὴν σύστασιν αὐτῷ καὶ οἷον οὐσίαν τῆς τοιαύτης ἐναντιώσεως φερούσης.[51]

> In the *logos* the conflict of the divergent elements rises within the one element, the Reason-Principle: the comparison therefore is rather with a harmony emerging directly from the conflicting elements themselves,[52] and the question becomes what introduces clashing elements among these Reason-Principles.[53] Now in the

[51] *Enn.* III 2, 16, 39-52.
[52] Cf. Eraclito B 8 DK.
[53] In this metaphor of harmony, the term for the relationships between musical notes is, indeed, λόγοι, which in Plotinus' conception are a specific manifestation of the universal *logos*.

> case of music, tones high and low are the product of Reason-Principles which, by the fact that they are Principles of harmony, meet in the unit of Harmony, the absolute Harmony, a more comprehensive Principle, greater than they and including them as its parts. Similarly in the Universe at large we find contraries-white and black, hot and cold, winged and wingless, footed and footless, reasoning and unreasoning- but all these elements are members of one living body, their sum-total; the Universe is a self-accordant entity,[54] its members everywhere clashing but the total being the manifestation of a Reason-Principle. That one Reason-Principle, then, must be the unification of conflicting Reason-Principles whose very opposition is the support of its coherence and, almost, of its Being.

In this symphonic system, to use the metaphor of the philosopher, no voice can produce a real dissonance. Those that may appear such, that is the evils (to be intended as the evil actions of free individuals), are to be considered used as the style effects of a composer (and conductor at the same time) with limitless abilities, as is the *logos*. But here Plotinus' construction clashes with the actual experience of the evils and with the Platonic teaching of the personal responsibility of *Resp.* X about the choice of life and consequently of the individual behaviors.

In the conclusion of the second treatise on providence, after returning several times on the issue, Plotinus elaborates a new metaphor based on the image of the root and the tree: from a single principle, in fact, he says that

> Πρόεισι δὲ ἤδη ἐκ ταύτης ἕκαστα μενούσης ἐκείνης ἔνδον οἷον ἐκ ῥίζης μιᾶς ἑστώσης αὐτῆς ἐν αὐτῇ· τὰ δὲ ἐξήνθησεν εἰς πλῆθος μεμερισμένον εἴδωλον ἕκαστον ἐκείνου φέρον, ἄλλο δὲ ἐν ἄλλῳ ἐνταῦθα ἤδη ἐγίγνετο καὶ ἦν τὰ μὲν πλησίον τῆς ῥίζης,

---

[54] Cf. Eraclito, fr. B 51 DK.

τὰ δὲ προιόντα εἰς τὸ πόρρω ἐσχίζετο καὶ μέχρις οἷον κλάδων καὶ ἄκρων καὶ καρπῶν καὶ φύλλων· καὶ τὰ μὲν ἔμενεν ἀεί, τὰ δὲ ἐγίνετο ἀεί, οἱ καρποὶ καὶ τὰ φύλλα· καὶ τὰ γινόμενα ἀεὶ εἶχε τοὺς τῶν ἐπάνω λόγους ἐν αὐτοῖς οἷον μικρὰ δένδρα βουληθέντα εἶναι, καὶ εἰ ἐγέννησε πρὶν φθαρῆναι, τὸ ἐγγὺς ἐγέννα μόνον. Τὰ δὲ διάκενα οἷον τῶν κλάδων ἐπληροῦτο ἐκ τῶν αὖ ἐκ τῆς ῥίζης καὶ αὐτῶν ἄλλον τρόπον πεφυκότων, ἐξ ὧν καὶ ἔπασχε τὰ ἄκρα τῶν κλάδων, ὡς ἐκ τοῦ πλησίον οἴεσθαι τὸ πάθος ἰέναι μόνον· τὸ δὲ κατὰ τὴν ἀρχὴν αὖ τὸ μὲν ἔπασχε, τὸ δὲ ἐποίει, ἡ δὲ ἀρχὴ ἀνήρτητο καὶ αὐτή. Πόρρωθεν μὲν γὰρ ἐλθόντα ἄλλα τὰ ποιοῦντα εἰς ἄλληλα, ἐξ ἀρχῆς δὲ ἀπὸ τοῦ αὐτοῦ, οἷον εἰ ἀδελφοὶ δρῷέν τι ἀλλήλους ὅμοιοι γενόμενοι ἐκ τῶν αὐτῶν ὁρμηθέντες τῶν πεποιηκότων.[55]

That which resumes all under a unity is a Principle in which all things exist together and the single thing is All. From this Principle, which remains internally unmoved, particular things push forth as from a single root which never itself emerges. They are a branching into part, into multiplicity, each single outgrowth bearing its trace of the common source. Thus, phase by phase, there in finally the production into this world; some things close still to the root, others widely separate in the continuous progression until we have, in our metaphor, bough and crest, foliage and fruit. At the one side all is one point of unbroken rest, on the other is the ceaseless process, leaf and fruit, all the things of process carrying ever within themselves the Reason-Principles of the Upper Sphere, and striving to become trees in their own minor order and producing, if at all, only what is in strict gradation from themselves. As for the abandoned spaces in what corresponds to the branches these two draw upon the root, from which, despite all their variance, they also derive; and the branches again operate upon their own furthest extremities: operation is to be traced only from point to next point, but, in the fact, there has been both inflow and outgo [of creative or modifying force] at the very root

[55] *Enn.* III 3, 7, 10-28.

> which, itself again, has its priors. The things that act upon each other are branchings from a far-off beginning and so stand distinct; but they derive initially from the one source: all interaction is like that of brothers, resemblant as drawing life from the same parents.

This metaphor, though grandiose, somehow seems to forget all contrasts, highlighting only the variety of beings. Would it be possible to apply it to men in their diversity? We might think that in Plotinus' intent this is valid for the diversity of characters and attitudes, which are not yet included in the field of moral freedom. Thus, the scope of individual autonomy seems once again to be in some way excluded from the general conception of the universe, at least in the two treatises on providence. The solution devised by Plotinus is to identify two types of relationship with respect to providence and therefore to necessity, one direct and the other indirect, both ultimately traced back to the same principle. To return to the passage from which we started, then, Idomeneus and Paris must be considered as brothers, however paradoxical it may seem on the ethical level.

A MOULD OF THE SOUL
REFLECTIONS ON AN AESTHETICS OF INTERIORS

An area that is still relatively unfamiliar from the academic point of view of applied aesthetics is that of interior design and decoration. There are some reasons why interior decoration in particular has not been considered worthy of scientific attention and, as is also true for other fields that could fall within aesthetic investigation, these reasons are linked to other issues, such as sociological and ethical for example, in particular in the continental tradition. Moreover, the very notion of decoration tends by its nature to be dismissed as secondary if not in itself morally wrong. However, what causes a certain confusion is also the blurred distinction between architecture and interior design, and between the latter and interior decoration, which even from the professional point of view still causes multiple discussions, and on which there is no specific common position on a global level.[1]

The aesthetics of architecture possesses nowadays its own clearer identity[2] and it certainly includes reflections on the aesthetic value of interiors. However, it often limits the discussion to certain aspects related to the value of public spaces or to the effect of the exterior of a building and it does not always

---

[1] In most countries there are imposed legal boundaries to what an interior designer can do in terms of interventions in a building compared to an architect or a structural engineer. An interesting exception to the general attitude to the philosophical approach to interiors is the institution of an International Doctorate in Philosophy of the Architectural Interior at the University of Naples "Federico II".

[2] See for example R. Scruton, *The Aesthetics of Architecture*, Princeton 2013^2 and K. Smith, (ed.), *Introducing Architectural Theory: Debating a Discipline*, New York 2012.

consider other elements such as the use of colour and materials which tend to be more specifically the realm of the interior designer's intervention. It must be recognised that the role of an interior designer does not have a fixed definition and can, depending on the different national contexts, be interchangeable with that of interior decorator. An accepted definition is that the interior designer addresses the way an interior works in terms of flow and is also in charge of devising certain aspects of joinery, lighting etc, while the role of the interior decorator is more cosmetic and is limited to the choice of paint, fabrics, wallpapers, and furniture. In some countries such as the United States of America and the United Kingdom the professions are even separated in the curricula of design schools. In practice, however, all these roles are rather more fluid and interior design and decoration constitues a particularly hybrid and non-fixed area and consequently an aesthetic reflection on interiors has to deal with the fact that the subject itself is prone to shifting meaning and scope.

However, if we consider that there is a specific industry of interiors, which includes designers, decorators, furniture and fabrics makers etc, it is more than legitimate to question from the point of view of aesthetics what the specific characteristics which lead to the appreciation of a certain interior are,[3] and in general the reflection on the value of interiors can certainly be related to the field of the so-called aesthetics of everyday. An interesting approach is that of considering aesthetic value and function not as opposite but as correlated in the experience of

---

[3] On the many features of an aesthetic experience, cf. H. Leder, B. Belke, A. Oeberst and D. Augustin, 'A Model of Aesthetic Appreciation and Aesthetic Judgments,' in *British Journal of Psychology*, 95,4 (2004), pp. 489–508. See also G. Iseminger, 'Aesthetic Appreciation,' in *The Journal of Aesthetics and Art Criticism* 39, 4 (1981), pp. 389-397.

aesthetic appreciation.[4] We must also consider that interior decoration in some ways is analogous to fashion, not only because it often follows certain trends but even more so because of the transient character of the decoration itself, which tends to be replaced with a certain frequency and mostly makes it impossible to define a time when a specific interior is really complete or is being altered or perfected, for example by the use that the inabitants make of it.

I would like to focus, for ease of discussion, on a definite aspect of interior design and decoration, that of residential interiors. It goes without saying that interiors have been the subject of studies from many angles, above all from the historical and sociological point of view but also from the literary one, and Mario Praz for example already in 1945 and then in 1964 had published his volume[5] on the evolution and the social motivations of the interior, which significantly had been given the Italian title of *Filosofia dell'arredamento*, inspired by E.A. Poe's title of *The Philosophy of Furniture*. As the whole field of residential interiors, however, is rather ample in the issues that it presents, I would like to draw attention to a category that is even more neglected than others which can more easily fall under the category of architecture: that is what could be described as classic or traditional interiors. I use this definition in the absence of a better one that can account for the extreme variety of stylistic expressions within this category, being aware that defining a certain interior as classic or even more traditional may induce a certain aversion which can be useful to address in our aesthetic reflection.

---

[4] Cf. G. Parsons and A. Carlson, *Functional Beauty*, Oxford 2008.

[5] M. Praz, *An Illustrated History of Interior Decoration from Pompeii to Art Nouveau*, London 1964.

The sociological and ethical problem

One of the reasons that perhaps has led to the neglect of some aspects of residential interior design within academic research arises from the fact that it cannot be easily defined and that some of the most celebrated interiors (at least among the ones that can be examined because images of them have been published) belong to high social classes and consequently a moral reaction is provoked against the very dignity of such an investigation. This is a real sociological, ideological and ethical issue[6] and it is important to be aware of the problems involved. In fact, much more than in the case of fashion, in our attitude towards a certain interior there seems to be a particular radicalization of choices, which tends to identify, for example, a modernistic interior with progressive values while a classical one can be considered as an expression of conservative and reactionary values. Certainly it can happen that this immediate identification shows some correspondence with the real choices and ideologies of the clients and designers of an interior, but one can also find many exceptions in which, for example, an interior with some traditional features belongs to an extremely unconventional figure with democratic political ideas, while some cutting-edge interiors can well belong to individuals with overall conservative values.

In order to define the type of interior that we will investigate, then, it is better to disregard such identification, but it is also useful to confute the assumption that good interiors can only be successful if supported by economic investments that the majority of people could not afford. There are in fact countless

---

[6] Cf. R. Stecker, 'The interaction of ethical and aesthetic value,' in *British Journal of Aesthetics*, 45, 2 (2005) 138-150.

examples that prove the opposite. Now, if fashion, despite its excesses and its extravagance, can be the subject of aesthetic investigation without the sociological aspect of it compromising its validity as object, this can also be implemented in the case of interior decoration. If fashion can be compared to poetry[7] and therefore be scrutinized from an aesthetic point of view, in the same way interior decoration can be compared to other synaesthetic art forms and be reviewed in an similar way. As in any other aspect of aesthetics of design, the complex interaction of different facets of the human and cultural reactions means that analysis has to take into consideration the results of psychology, consumer psychology, marketing and advertising, and many more areas of research – a task that often burdens those who try to address an aesthetic issue.

Interior design as an industry with its peculiarities

The other central element for the need to establish interior design and decoration as an object of aesthetic investigation is its presence in everyday life as the cause and inspiration of a certain pleasure. A specialized industry, which involves a variety of manufacturers and artisans and has designers as active players, is driven, like fashion, by a selection of influential magazines. This in itself would be enough to make interior decoration worthy of aesthetic attention and also to differentiate it from architecture, to which it is similar in many aspects but from which it differs in many others. In particular, interior design and decoration has to do with internal space, with the

---

[7] See R.G. Saisselin, 'From Baudelaire to Christian Dior: The Poetics of Fashion,' in *The Journal of Aesthetics and Art Criticism* 18, 1 (1959), 109-115, which however is rather dated in defining fashion as poetry of femininity, as this definition can apply to both genders.

circulation and the various functions of living, but considers them from a different point of view than architecture,[8] and this is particularly true in those interiors that we could call classic and that make use of a notable series of decorative artifices in which a contemporary architect would rarely be interested. For example, the tactile use of fabrics becomes a specialism of the decorator, who is aware of the different textural properties of a fabric and chooses it for a series of aesthetic reasons in the original meaning of the term, that is, for the effect on the senses, from touch to sight. In this sense, the experience of an interior can be intensely aesthetic because it surrounds those who are in it by investing them with sensory stimuli which in normal conditions appear as pleasant. Many of the most successful interiors also resort to the synaesthetic process and reach the user through multiple senses, including, beyond sight and touch, also the sound quality or the scent of a place. Even a garden assumes these qualities, and in fact home and garden form a combination often used by the specialized magazines themselves, but in the case of the interior the designer's control of the aesthetic experience can be much tighter, due to the necessarily more artificial context of indoor conditions.[9]

Colour, shape, tactile qualities, vibrations of sound are all elements inherent in interior design and decoration, and each of them can be the object of a specific aesthetic analysis. Interior design, therefore, by its very nature, is a complex field

---

[8] Cf. J. Young Cho and B. Schwarz, 'Aesthetic Theory and Interior Design Pedagogy,' in J.A. Asher Thompson and N. Blossom (edd.), *The Handbook of Interior Design*, Chichester 2015, pp. 478-496.

[9] For the manipulation of the aesthetic experience of commercial spaces, cf. M. Sloane, 'Tuning the Space: Investigating the Making of Atmospheres through Interior Design Practices,' in *Interiors. Design/ Architecture/ Culture* 5, 3 (2014), pp. 297-314.

that raises many questions about its aesthetic validity and the reasons why one could say that an interior has certain qualities or not. In some ways, the various forms of aesthetic experience[10] that can be produced in the design and decoration of an interior can be compared to the design of a set. However, in the case of set design usually only the visual experience is involved, as also happens when an interior is observed through a photographic reproduction. The most successful interiors, instead, are a combination of aesthetic sensations and can be fully appreciated only by being in them.[11]

In this sense, we can certainly include interior design in a more general reflection on the specificity of the aesthetic experience related to design. On the other hand, however, in interiors as in other creative forms, such as music, which most directly affect emotions, the emotional aspect of the experience is to be considered part of the aesthetic enjoyment[12] and not as an external element. The way in which, to consider a very basic example, a fabric produces a pleasant effect has to do with previous cognitive experiences, as well as with profound cultural reactions. For this reason, at the same mild temperature, those who grew up in cold climates may have a reaction of pleasure at the contact with the texture of a thick woollen fabric, while those who are accustomed to warm climates may have a feeling of rejection, due to associations with previous experiences. The same may happen with food or

---

[10] N. Carroll, 'Aesthetic Experience Revisited,' in *The British Journal of Aesthetics* 42, 2 2002, pp. 145–168.

[11] See K. Pint, 'The experience of the interior: outlines of an alternative anthropology,' in *Interiors. Design/ Architecture/ Culture* 7, 1 (2016), pp. 55-72.

[12] A different point of view in P. Hekkert, 'Design aesthetics: principles of pleasure in design,' in *Psychology Science* 48, 2 (2006), p. 157-172.

smells. On the other hand, the individual reaction will follow different dynamics depending on whether or not it identifies with the dominant type of a civilization. In this sense, the convincing theory of mirror neurons and of the empathetic response based in the brain[13] inevitably needs to consider the interaction of other socio-cultural elements in the formation of an aesthetic experience. Another criterion related to cognitive science, that of familiarity,[14] could be seen as having a dominant function for interiors as much as for fashion, and in the dialectic between familiarity and the search for the new, inevitably, lies the key to many of the historical alternatives of taste.

A case study: Renzo Mongiardino

Among the many authoritative designers and decorators who are recognized worldwide as tastemakers, I would like to focus on a specific example as it presents some remarkable features compared to the work of other practitioners, as it makes a competent use of two specific concepts that introduce a further level compared to the simply sensorial ones to which we referred so far: these concepts are those of atmosphere[15] and memory. With these terms we can specifically reconnect the work of the architect, designer and decorator Renzo Mongiardino (1916-1998), due to its cultured and literary di-

---

[13] See D. Freedberg and V. Gallese, 'Motion, emotion and empathy in aesthetic experience trends,' in *Cognitive Sciences* 11, 5 (2007), pp. 197-203.
[14] Cf. J.N. Howe, 'Familiarity and no Pleasure. The Uncanny as an Aesthetic Emotion,' in *Image & Narrative* 11, 3 (2010), pp. 42-63. See also D.A. Norman, *Emotional Design: Why We Love (or Hate) Everyday Things*, New York 2004.
[15] See T. Griffero, 'Dal bello all'atmosferico tra estetica e atmosferologia,' in L. Russo (ed.), *Dopo l'estetica*, Palermo 2015, pp. 133-146.

mension which is able to produce an emotion perhaps indefinite but real, giving an interior a dynamic suggestion which needs specific understanding by its user because of its numerous and almost arcane cultural associations.

Born in Genoa, Renzo Mongiardino became one of the most sought-after designers in the international jet-set, with clients such as the Agnellis and Rothschilds as well as prominent fashion designers. The interiors designed by Mongiardino are deliberately inspired by the past and based on a series of decorative choices that strongly oppose current trends, and his clients, inevitably, must have been independent personalities who did not fear the resolutely unfashionable effect of their homes. The decisive rejection of contemporary solutions is combined with a skill in the recreation of an indefinite memory of the past also due to the experience of Mongiardino as a set designer for theatre and cinema. In his book *Roomscapes*, a survey of some of his design principles, he wrote some illuminating pages on his own way of interpreting the creation of interiors and the emotions and atmosphere that these can evoke, as he lucidly illustrates:

> I understood that everything in our lives takes place within a space that surrounds us, therefore within architecture [...]. All we do is imitate, remake, re-create that which nature and history offer us.[16]

Today, the interest of the design milieu in Mongiardino's interiors, after more than a decade of neglect, is suddenly growing again and he has been recently the subject of an exhibition of

---

[16] R. Mongiardino, *Roomscapes*, New York 2016^2, p. 18.

his sketches in Milan[17] and of two monographs,[18] while his own monograph has been republished.

An example of particular interest [*fig. 1*] in explaining how his architectural approach has more to do with atmosphere than with spatial efficiency is the expedient that Mongiardino used on two occasions to transform an attic space into something different, evoking strong literary connotations aimed at recreating, in a Milanese interior, the feeling of being in Russia in the mid-nineteenth century:

> *Any attic space, which, at first glance, might seem difficult to resolve and limited in possibilities, can sometimes favour invention and lead to unexpected decisions. This space was exceedingly large and obstinately low. I could have raised the ceiling, reclaiming some airspace. The center of the space had sufficient height, but at the sides the pitch of the roof reached right down to the floor. To use the center, filling the sides with wardrobes and bookshelves, and to replace the reinforced concrete beams and simulate a joist-and-beam structure, would have been a solution that easily satisfied a taste for the "rustic". I wanted to avoid this [...]. The solution became clear with a recollection: a Russian tempera painting of 1840. [...] A barrel vault was traced, and the curve rested on the wanscoting of the room. On two sides, the windows, like slits in the curve of a tunnel, created shafts of light and shadow. The room's only supporting walls were the two at the entrance and along the back; these were the only places to put a fireplace, as well as the furniture and a large painting. The "scenery" was all brought to the center, and an imposing square*

[17] See T. Tovaglieri (ed.), *Omaggio a Renzo Mongiardino (1916-1998) architetto e scenografo. Catalogo della mostra (Milano, 28 settembre-11 dicembre 2016)* Milan 2016.

[18] L. Verchère, *Renzo Mongiardino: Renaissance Master of Style*, New York 2013; M. Mondadori Sartogo, *The Interiors and Architecture of Renzo Mongiardino: A Painterly Vision*, New York 2017.

> *table-bookshelf divided the room lenghtwise. But the true protagonist of the space was the ceiling, which extended almost down to the floor. It was decorated with a skillful illusion of rosette-shaped coffering, ranging in hue from ivory to olive green and ending at a darker wainscoting, which reinforced the enveloping effect of the large mansard.*[19]

The adoption of a bold and unusual solution, such as renouncing the effective use of part of the floor area in order to accentuate the atmospheric effect, produces a constriction of the space that must have an effect, for some claustrophobic and for others dizzying, considering that those standing in this space are in direct contact with a vault and consequently may have the feeling that, in a normal architecture, they are at a considerable height from the floor. It is an interior emotionally invested, where the impact of architecture is not based only on the elements of colour and texture but owes its effect precisely to the cultural connections that it activates. The choice of colours, in this context, is secondary, as the effect could be equally obtained in grisaille, however it intensifies the architectural anomaly of the room.

---

[19] R. Mongiardino, *Roomscapes*, cit., p. 49.

Fig. 1: A barrel-vaulted drawing room in a Milanese interior by Renzo Mongiardino. Illustration by the author.

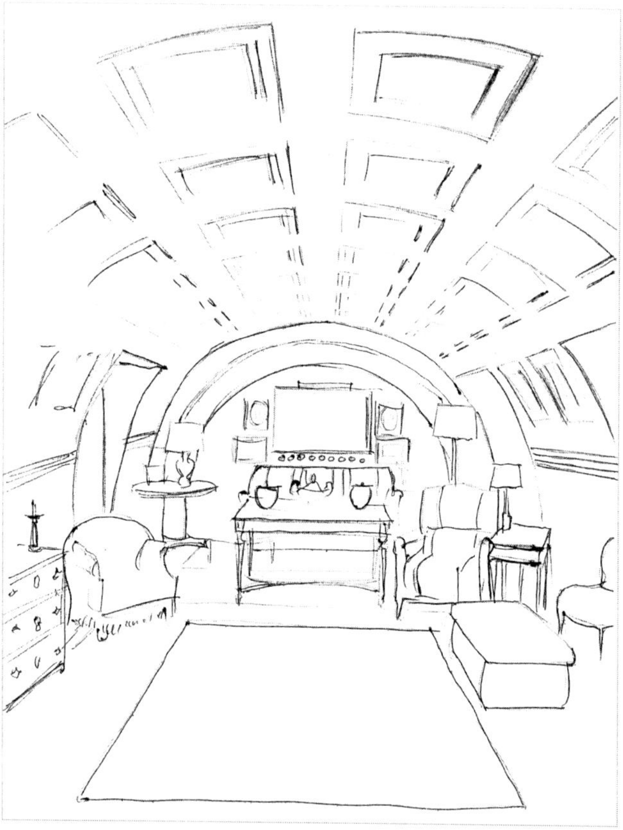

Fig. 2: A dining room in a Milanese interior by Renzo Mongiardino. Illustration by the author.

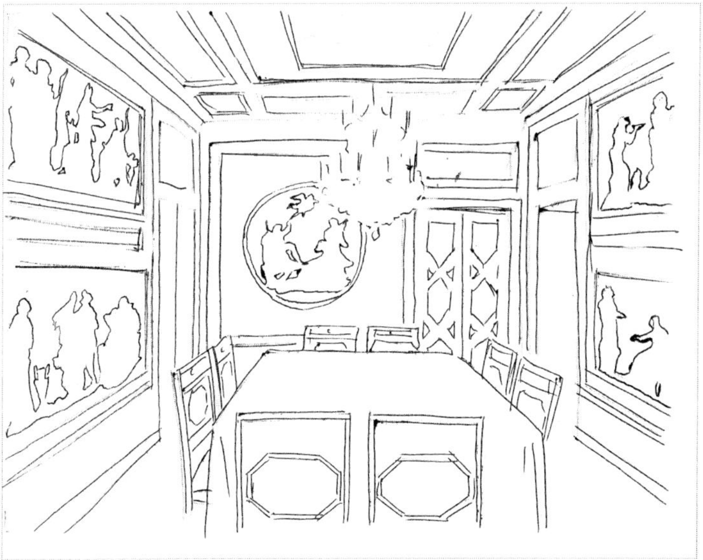

Fig. 3: A bathroom in the Château de Wideville, by Renzo Mongiardino. Illustration by the author.

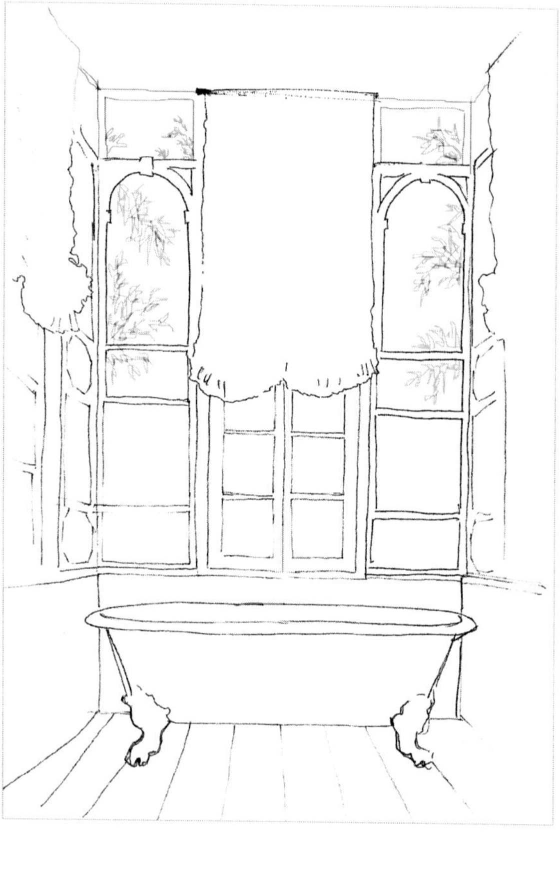

Inevitably, in order to enjoy such individual interiors, the client must have the same kind of sensitivity and cultural references and, consequently, the choice of a designer such as Mongiardino is based mainly on cultural affinity and on the sharing of specific aesthetic choices, not necessarily confined to interior decoration. It seems to be sometimes the case for clients to choose a designer in order to raise their social status, however if the designer is, like Mongiardino, strongly imbued with a cultured literary, historical and philosophical inspiration, it is less likely that he or she would be commissioned by clients who do not appreciate and even more share the same cultural matrix, with the foreseeable corollary that their choice intensifies their identification as patrons and intellectuals.

A second example [*fig. 2*] that can be considered, this time to understand how the decorative transformation can alter the perception of a space, again with the insertion of the cultured reference to a neoclassical inspiration, is, in the same apartment in Milan in which Mongiardino created one of his barrel-vaulted drawing rooms, the construction of a dining room within an space without symmetry and architectural interest. Through use of Neapolitan wooden panels of the second half of the eighteenth century, he infused structure to a room of limited size that posed many decorative difficulties due to the position of doors and windows and in general the lack of prominent features, apart form its square shape. With the insertion of a false door but above all thanks to the adoption of wooden panels as the only decorative element inside a cage of lines, Mongiardino obtained a dramatic and at the same time welcoming result, and he conferred historical and artistic dignity to a featureless interior, transforming it into a treasure chest full of mythological and literary references. As he explains:

> *The result was a compact composition, in which every decorative element framed within the overall structure formed an architecture without repose, a tight weave, within which the smallness of the room remained imprisoned in a new casing.*
> *Reconstructed, almost deconstructed, the new, invented proportion achieved a certain harmony.*[20]

A last example [*fig. 3*], among the many possible, of Mongiardino's mastery at transforming the architectural limitations of a space into the opportunity to create an aesthetic experience for those using it, is a relatively small bathroom in one of the corner towers of the Château de Wideville outside Paris, an early seventeenth century building. Here the room presented extreme challenges, as its floor dimensions are 180x180 cm, therefore just big enough for a full functioning bathroom, while its imposing height, due to the architecture of the chateau, is 5 metres. Moreover, three tall windows and a door caused further limitations to the use of the space, and for this reason Mongiardino chose not to fight against the awkward dimensions of the room, embracing instead its peculiarity in order to create an unexpected sensorial experience. Above a marble wainscoting he covered the walls between the windows with mirrors right up to a domed ceiling, itself mirrored, with a nod to the the painted mirrors of the Baroque artist Mario dei Fiori. The overall effect was that of real and painted greenery merged together on the walls of the bathroom:

> Here, there was no gleam through the darkness (*unlike the patina on the paintings on mirror by Mario dei Fiori*); on the contrary, there was total light in which the real woods were reflected in the

[20] Ib., p. 43.

> mirror, giving the feeling that one could bathe in an empty cage, among the trees.[21]

To this it must be added that the main feature of the room, as in all the other interiors by Mongiardino, is the overall historicism of the invention, in the sense that the room has a distinctively eighteenth century feel to it, reminiscent, for example, of the delicate naturalism of the so-called room of Voltaire at Sanssoucci, however without copying any specific element of it. Again, only a highly educated client could understand the erudite cultural references of the design.

These three examples give an insight into the way designers can manipulate space and ambiance creating a new experience, something that an architect (as Mongiardino was) could certainly do but that is the peculiar aspect of the activity of an interior designer and decorator. It must be mentioned that, in less talented hands, such extravagant interventions often result in aesthetic disasters, and that is what happens when designers and clients are unaware of, for example, the proportions of the classical orders. The sad results of a poor imitation game can be seen everywhere and give traditional interior decoration the bad reputation of being pastiche, stuffy and ridiculous. At the other end of the spectrum, it must also be said that the handling of minimalism or of ironic approach in interiors by incompetent designers often results too in uncomfortable or unlivable spaces.

---

[21] Ib., p. 63.

Conclusions

The peculiarity of interior design and decoration as a form of art is that it produces spaces to live in, which are constantly worn, changed and altered and often are the result of a compromise between the creative vision of the designer and the taste and preferences of the client. It is true that historically the decisions of the committents have had an impact on the artworks that most artists created, so in this sense interiors are not necessarily different from other artistic productions. What is distinctive, even more than in set design, which is very similar and in fact has been sometimes practiced by interior designers, is the fact that the talented professional creates an interior which exists not only in its individual elements, the furniture or the upholstery or the colours or the lighting, but also relies on atmosphere. This atmosphere is produced by the combination of the elements of the design with the addition of other ones that are less obvious, such as smells, the sensation of warmth or coolness depending on the climate and the weather, the liveness or privacy of the space, and all those who experience the interior respond to these components in a different way, depending on cultural associations but also on subconscious reactions.

Incidentally, the alliance of such diverse components cannot be captured by photography, which inevitably is the main medium for the study of interiors, but can only be perceived in the actual space. That is why, when certain photographs, like those by Horst P. Horst, can capture the accidents of sunlight or the movement of curtains in the summer breeze, they convey by association a little bit more of the spirit and ambiance of a place than the perfect stillness of an ordinary interior magazine photograph. The elusiveness of atmosphere brings us to a last reflection: if we consider both the individual features and the overall ambiance of a successful domestic interior, and the need to experience it in order to understand it, it could even be said that there are similarities with art installations. The main difference is the purpose of an interior, which is not to be experienced within a codified ritual, but to be lived in, mostly interacting with other people and often in a non-conscious way.

Mario Praz, in his introduction to *La filosofia dell'arredamento*, describes the traumatising experience of the Second World War and its scars on the domestic interiors:

> At Viterbo's Roman Gate, the magic screen of memory was brutally torn away, and your mind was gripped by rubble, destruction, and horror. The visitor couldn't proceed, or had to force his way forward over an uncertain, despoiled terrain, crossed by the impotent track of a little narrow-gauge railroad. "There are still four hundred victims here," you were told at the Florentine Gate, and wherever you looked, you could see only shattered, ruined buildings, the hollow orbits of windows, and fragments of walls, houses split in two, with the pathetic sight of some still furbished corner, dangling above the rubble, surrounded by ruin: pictures hanging on broken walls, a kitchen with the pots still on the stove and there, in what must once have been a drawing-room, a sofa. Like a collage by Max Ernst, a bed in a boudoir is grazed by the furious waves of a stormy sea; or an abyss yawns at the foot of the most ordinary middle-class dining room; so reality had decided to make the Surrealist's mad fantasy come true.[22]

The excruciating subversion of the intimacy of interiors highlights, by contrast, their natural necessity. Praz theorizes the function of the well appointed room of a collector who, in-

[22] M. Praz, *An Illustrated History of Interior Decoration*, cit., p. 17.

stinctively, designs a room for himself, in the Narcissistic act of controlling the space around him:

> The surroundings become a museum of the soul, an archive of its experiences; it reads in them its own history, and is perennially conscious of itself; the surroundings are the resonance chamber where its strings render their authentic vibration. And just as many pieces of furniture are like moulds of the human body, empty forms waiting to receive it, [...] so finally the whole room or apartment becomes a mould of the spirit, the case without which the soul would feel like a snail without its shell.[23]

This very individual need is not, however, found in every interior and, as the writer himself wittily acknowledges, there are many who don't feel any need at all to take aesthetic care of their surroundings. Also, it can happen that the client delegates to the professional the entire conception of a room, which can be successful and meaningful even if those who actually use it were little involved in its design. Nevertheless, the validity of Praz's reflections lies in the recognition of the interior as a reality worthy of aesthetical discussion, a shell created as a pleasant, comfortable and artful background for the activities of its inhabitants, almost a *Gesamtkunstwerk* for domestic life.

---

[23] Ib. pp. 24-25.

Bibliography

Acosta-Hughes, B., L. Lehnus and S. Stephens (edd.), *Brill's Companion to Callimachus*, Brill 2011.

Acosta-Hughes, B. and S. Stephens, *Callimachus in Context*, Cambridge 2012.

Allen, M.J.B., *Synoptic Art: Marsilio Ficino on the History of Platonic Interpretation, Firenze* 1998.

Allen, M.J.B., and V. Rees, with M. Davies, *Marsilio Ficino: his Theology, his Philosophy, his Legacy*, Leiden-Boston 2002.

Ardissino, E., *Tasso, Plotino, Ficino. In margine a un postillato*, Roma 2003.

Armstrong, A.H., *The Architecture of the Intelligible Universe in the Philosophy of Plotinus*, Cambridge 1949.

Basta Donzelli, G., 'La colpa di Elena. Gorgia ed Euripide a confronto,' in L. Montoneri-F. Romano, *Gorgia e la Sofistica*, Atti del Convegno Internazionale di Lentini-Catania, 12-15 dicembre 1983, Catania 1985, pp. 389-409, repr. in Ead., *Studi sul teatro antico*, Amsterdam 2008, pp. 137-150.

Basta Donzelli, G., 'La seconda giovinezza di Callimaco (fr.1, 32 ss. Pf.),' in *Studi di Filologia Classica in onore di G. Monaco*, vol. I, Palermo 1991, 387-394.

Blondell, R., *Helen of Troy: Beauty, Myth, Devastation*, Oxford 2015.

Bobzien, S., 'The Inadvertent Conception and Late Birth of the Free-Will Problem,' in *Phronesis* XLIII (1998), pp. 133-175.

Boys-Stones, G., 'Middle Platonists on Fate and Human Autonomy,' in R.W. Sharples-R. Sorabji (edd.), *Greek and Roman Philosophy from 100 BC to 200 AD*, London, pp. 431-447.

Brink, K.O., 'Callimachus and Aristotle: An Inquiry into Callimachus' 'ΠΡΟΣ ΠΡΑΞΙΦΑΝΗΝ',' *Classical Quarterly* 40, 1946, 11-26.

Bulloch, A.W., 'Hellenistic Poetry,' in P.E. Easterling, E.J. Kenney, B.M.W. Knox, M.V. Clausen (edd.), *The Cambridge History of Classical Literature, vol. I: Greek Literature*, Cambridge 1985, 541-621.

Burke, P., *The Fortunes of the Courtier: The European Reception of Castiglione's* Cortegiano, Cambridge 2007[3].

Cardullo, R.L., *Il linguaggio del simbolo in Proclo: analisi filosofico-semantica dei termini symbolon/eikôn/synthêma nel 'Commentario alla Repubblica'*, Catania 1985.

Carroll, N., 'Aesthetic Experience Revisited,' in *The British Journal of Aesthetics* 42, 2 2002, pp. 145–168.

Castelfranchi Vegas, L., *L'Angelico e l'Umanesimo*, Milano 1989.

Clayman, D.L., *Timon of Phlius: Pyrrhonism into Poetry*, Berlin-New York 2009.

Clements, R.J., *Michelangelo's Theory of Art*, New York 1961.

Couloubaritsis, L., 'Le Logos hénologique chez Plotin,' in M.O. Goulet-Cazé, G. Madec, D. O'Brien (edd.), *ΣΟΦΙΗΣ ΜΑΙΗΤΟΡΕΣ. Chercheurs de Sagesse. Hommage à Jean Pépin*, Paris 1992, pp. 231-243.

D'Alessio, G.B. (ed.), *Callimaco: Inni; Epigrammi; Ecale; Aitia; Giambi e altri frammenti*, Milano 2007[4].

D'Angelo, P., *Sprezzatura: Concealing the Effort of Art from Aristotle to Duchamp*, New York 2018.

Dekel, E., *Virgil's Homeric Lens*, New York-London 2012.

Destreé, P., 'Pleasure,' in P. Destreé and P. Murray (edd.), *Blackwell Companion to Ancient Aesthetics*, Chichester 2015, 472-485.

Di Pasquale Barbanti, M., and C. Martello (eds.), *Neoplatonismo pagano vs. Neoplatonismo cristiano. Identità e intersezioni*, atti del Seminario Internazionale di Catania, 25-26 Settembre 2004, Catania 2006.

Eliasson, E., *The Notion of* That Which Depends on Us *in Plotinus and Its Background*, Leiden-Boston 2008.

Emison, P.A., *Creating the "Divine" Artist: From Dante to Michelangelo*, Leiden 2004.

Exum, J.K., *Tragedy and Biblical Narrative,* Cambridge 1992.

Fabian, K., *Callimaco. 'Aitia' II: testo critico, traduzione e commento*, Alessandria 1992.

Freedberg, D., and V. Gallese, 'Motion, emotion and empathy in aesthetic experience trends,' in *Cognitive Sciences* 11, 5 (2007), pp. 197-203.

Garulli, V., 'Cleombroto di Ambracia e il "Lector in fabula" in Callimaco (Call. '*Epigr.*' 23 Pf.),' *Lexis* 25, 2007, pp. 325-336.

Griffero, T., 'Dal bello all'atmosferico tra estetica e atmosferologia,' in L. Russo (ed.), *Dopo l'estetica*, Palermo 2015, pp. 133-146.

Gutzwiller, K., 'The Nautilus, the Halycon, and Selenaia: Callimachus's *Epigram* 5 Pf. = 14 G. – P,' in *Classical Antiquity* 11, 1992, pp. 194-209.

Hadley, D., and S. Hutton, (eds.), *Platonism at the Origins of Modernity. Studies on Platonism and Early Modern Philosophy*, Dordrecht 2008.

Harder, A. (ed.), *Callimachus, 'Aetia'*, Oxford 2012.

Hawkins, T., *Iambic Poetics in the Roman Empire*, Cambridge 2014.

Hekkert, P., 'Design aesthetics: principles of pleasure in design,' in *Psychology Science* 48, 2 (2006), p. 157-172.

Henry, P., and H.R. Schwyzer (edd.), *Plotini Opera* (*editio minor*), Oxford 1964-1982.

Howe, J.N., 'Familiarity and no Pleasure. The Uncanny as an Aesthetic Emotion,' in *Image & Narrative* 11, 3 (2010), pp. 42-63.

Iozzia, D., 'Il carattere ossimorico delle emozioni d'amore in Plotino, *Enn.* I 6 (1) 4, 15-17,' in G.R. Giardina (ed.), *Le emozioni secondo i filosofi antichi*, Catania 2008, pp. 163-175.

Iozzia, D., *Plotino. La provvidenza. Enn. III 2 e III 3*, Roma 2009.

Iozzia, D., *Aesthetic Themes in Pagan and Christian Neoplatonism*, London 2015.

Iseminger, G., 'Aesthetic Appreciation,' in *The Journal of Aesthetics and Art Criticism* 39, 4 (1981), pp. 389-397.

Janko, R., (ed.), *Philodemus, 'On Poems' I*, Oxford 2003.

Kraye, G., 'The Transformation of Platonic Love in the Italian Renaissance,' in A. Baldwin and S. Hutton (eds.), *Platonism and the English Imagination*, Cambridge 1994, pp. 76-85.

Kuisma, O., *Art or Experience: a study on Plotinus' Aesthetics*, Helsinki 2003.

Lampe, K., *The Birth of Hedonism: The Cyrenaic Philosophers and Pleasure as a Way of Life*, Princeton, 2015.

Leder, H., B. Belke, A. Oeberst and D. Augustin, 'A Model of Aesthetic Appreciation and Aesthetic Judgments,' in *British Journal of Psychology*, 95,4 (2004), pp. 489–508.

Leroux. G. (ed.), *Plotin. Traité sur la liberté et la volonté de l'Un*, Paris 1990.

Linguiti, A., 'La materia dei corpi: sullo pseudoilomorfismo plotiniano,' in *Quaestio* 7 (2007), pp. 105-122.

Lobsien, O., and C. Olk (eds.), *Neuplatonismus und Äesthetik. Zur Transformationsgeschichte des Schönen*, Berlin-New York 2007.

Massimilla, G. (ed.), *Callimaco, 'Aitia': Libri Primo e Secondo*, Pisa 1996.

Massimilla, G. (ed.), *Callimaco, 'Aitia': Libri Terzo e Quarto*, Pisa/Roma 2010.

Meillier, C., *Callimaque et son temp*, Lille 1979.

Mondadori Sartogo, M., *The Interiors and Architecture of Renzo Mongiardino: A Painterly Vision*, New York 2017.

Mongiardino, R., *Roomscapes*, New York 2016[2].

Muccillo, M., 'Plotino nel tardo Rinascimento,' in Ead., *Platonismo, ermetismo e «prisca theologia». Ricerche di storiografia filosofica rinascimentale*, Firenze 1996, pp. 195-289.

Murray, P., 'Poetic Inspiration,' in P. Murray and P. Destrée (edd.), *Blackwell Companion to Ancient Aesthetics*, Chichester 2015, pp. 158-174.

Norman, D.A., *Emotional Design: Why We Love (or Hate) Everyday Things*, New York 2004.

O'Brien, D., 'Comment écrivait Plotin? Étude sur la *Vie de Plotin* 8. 1-4,' dans Porphyre, *La Vie de Plotin I*, ed. by L. Brisson et al., Paris 1982, pp. 329–368.

Opsomer, J., 'The Middle Platonic doctrine of conditional fate,' in P. d'Hoine and G. Van Riel (edd.), *Fate, Providence and moral responsibility in Ancient, Medieval and Early Modern thought*, Leuven 2014, pp. 137-168.

Panofsky, E., *Idea. A Concept in Art Theory*, Columbia, SC. 1968.

Parsons, G., and A. Carlson, *Functional Beauty*, Oxford 2008.

Perry, E.E., 'Notes on Diligentia as a Term of Roman Art Criticism,' in *Classical Philology*, 95, 4 (2000), pp. 445-458.

Pfeiffer, R. (ed.), *Callimachus, vol. I: Fragmenta*, Oxford 1949.

Pint, K., 'The experience of the interior: outlines of an alternative anthropology,' in *Interiors. Design/ Architecture/ Culture* 7, 1 (2016), pp. 55-72.

Praz, M., *An Illustrated History of Interior Decoration from Pompeii to Art Nouveau*, London 1964.

Ready, J.N., *Character, Narrator, and Simile in the* Iliad, Cambridge 2011.

Rist, J., *Plotinus. The Road to Reality*, Cambridge 1967.

Romano, A.J., 'Callimachus and Contemporary Criticism,' in B. Acosta-Hughes, L. Lehnus, S. Stephens (edd.), *Brill's Companion to Callimachus*, cit., pp. 309-328.

Romano, F., 'Azione morale e libero arbitrio in Plotino. "La virtù non ha padrone" [ἀρετὴ ἀδέσποτον] (Plat., *Rep.* X, 617e 3),' in M. Vegetti e M. Abbate (edd.), *La* Repubblica *di Platone nella tradizione antica*, Napoli 1999, pp. 151-191.

Saffrey, H.D., 'Pourquoi Porphyre a-t-il édité Plotin? Réponse provisoire,' in Porphyre, *La Vie de Plotin. II: Études d'introduction, texte grec et traduction française, commentaire, notes complémentaires, bibliographie*, ed. L. Brisson et al., Paris 1992, pp. 31-64.

Saisselin, R.G., 'From Baudelaire to Christian Dior: The Poetics of Fashion,' in *The Journal of Aesthetics and Art Criticism* 18, 1 (1959), 109-115.

Scruton, R., *The Aesthetics of Architecture*, Princeton 2013^2.

Serrano, C.M., 'Facilità y non finito en las vidas de Vasari,' in *EGA: revista de expresión gráfica arquitectónica* 9 (2004), pp. 58-67.

Sharples, R.W., 'The Stoic Background to the Middle Platonist Discussion of Fate,' in M. Bonazzi-Ch. Helmig (edd.), *Platonic Stoicism – Stoic Platonism. The Dialogue between Platonism and Stoicism in Antiquity*, Leuven 2008, pp. 169-188.

Sheppard, A., *Studies on the 5th and 6th Essays of Proclus' Commentary on the 'Republic'*, Göttingen 1980.

Sloane, M., 'Tuning the Space: Investigating the Making of Atmospheres through Interior Design Practices,' in *Interiors. Design/ Architecture/ Culture* 5, 3 (2014), pp. 297-314.

Smith, K., (ed.), *Introducing Architectural Theory: Debating a Discipline*, New York 2012.

Spike, T., *Angelico*, Milano 1996.

Stecker, R., 'The interaction of ethical and aesthetic value,' in *British Journal of Aesthetics*, 45, 2 (2005) 138-150.

Summers, D., *Michelangelo and the Language of Arts*, Princeton 1981.

Szlezák, T.A., *Platone e Aristotele nella dottrina del* Nous *di Plotino*, Milano 1997.

Tovaglieri, T., (ed.), *Omaggio a Renzo Mongiardino (1916-1998) architetto e scenografo. Catalogo della mostra (Milano, 28 settembre-11 dicembre 2016)* Milan 2016.

Tsouna, V., *The Epistemology of the Cyrenaic School*, Cambridge 1998.

Tsouna, V., 'Cyrenaics and Epicureans on Pleasure and the Good Life: The Original Debate and Its Later Revivals,' in S. Weisser and N. Thaler (edd.), *Strategies of Polemics in Greek and Roman Philosophy*, Leiden 2016, pp. 113-49.

Valverde Sánchez, M., 'El mito de Idomeneo, de la épica antigua a la tragedia moderna,' in *Myrtia* XX (2005), pp. 265-291.

Verchère, L., *Renzo Mongiardino: Renaissance Master of Style*, New York 2013

White, S.A., *Callimachus on Plato and Cleombrotus*, TAPhS 124, 1994, pp. 135-161.

Young Cho, J., and B. Schwarz, 'Aesthetic Theory and Interior Design Pedagogy,' in J.A. Asher Thompson and N. Blossom (edd.), *The Handbook of Interior Design*, Chichester 2015, pp. 478-496.

Zilioli, U., *The Cyrenaics*, Durham 2012.